UNREASONED VERDICT

The system of jury trial has survived, intact, for 750 years. In the light of contemporary opposition to jury trial for serious offences, this book explains the nature and scope today of jury trial, with its minor exceptions. It chronicles the origins and development of jury trial in the Anglo-Saxon world, seeking to explain and explore the principles that lie at the heart of the mode of criminal trial. It observes the distinction between the professional judge and the amateur juror or lay participant, and the value of such a mixed tribunal. Part of the book is devoted to the leading European jurisdictions, underlining their abandonment of trial by jury and its replacement with the mixed tribunal in pursuance of a political will to inject a lay element into the trial process. Democracy is not an essential element in the criminal trial. The book examines the appellate system in crime, from the Criminal Appeals Act 1907 to the present day, and urges the reform of the appellate court, finding the trial decision unsatisfactory as well as unsafe. Other important issues are touched upon – judicial ethics and court-craft; perverse jury verdicts (the nullification of jury verdicts); the speciality of fraud offences, and the selection of models for various crimes, as well as suggested reforms of the waiver of a jury trial or the ability of the defendant to choose the mode of trial. The section ends with a discussion of the restricted exceptions to jury trial, where the experience of 30 years of judge-alone trials in Northern Ireland – the Diplock Courts – is discussed. Finally, the book proffers its proposal for a major change in direction – involvement of the defendant in the choice of mode of trial, and the intervention (where necessary) of the expert, not merely as a witness but as an assessor to the judiciary or as a supplemental decision-maker.

Unreasoned Verdict

The Jury's Out

Louis Blom-Cooper

·HART·

OXFORD · LONDON · NEW YORK · NEW DELHI · SYDNEY

HART PUBLISHING

Bloomsbury Publishing Plc

Kemp House, Chawley Park, Cumnor Hill, Oxford, OX2 9PH, UK

HART PUBLISHING, the Hart/Stag logo, BLOOMSBURY and the Diana logo are
trademarks of Bloomsbury Publishing Plc

First published in Great Britain 2019

A catalogue record for this book is available from the British Library.

Library of Congress Cataloging-in-Publication data

Names: Blom-Cooper, Louis, 1926–2018, author.

Title: Unreasoned verdict : the jury's out / Louis Blom-Cooper.

Description: Oxford, UK ; Chicago, Illinois : Hart Publishing, 2019. |
Includes bibliographical references and index.

Identifiers: LCCN 2019006350 (print) | LCCN 2019007751 (ebook) |
ISBN 9781509915248 (EPub) | ISBN 9781509915224 (hardback)

Subjects: LCSH: Jury—England. | Jury. | BISAC: LAW / Criminal Procedure.

Classification: LCC KD8400 (ebook) | LCC KD8400 .B57 2019 (print) |
DDC 347.42/0752—dc23

LC record available at https://lccn.loc.gov/2019006350

ISBN: HB: 978-1-50991-522-4
        ePDF: 978-1-50991-523-1
        ePub: 978-1-50991-524-8

Typeset by Compuscript Ltd, Shannon
Printed and bound in Great Britain by CPI Group (UK) Ltd, Croydon CR0 4YY

MIX
Paper from
responsible sources
FSC® C013604

To find out more about our authors and books visit www.hartpublishing.co.uk.
Here you will find extracts, author information, details of forthcoming events
and the option to sign up for our newsletters.

Contents

Table of Cases

Tables of Statutes

Table of Statutory Instruments etc

Table of EU and International material

Table of National Legislation

AUSTRALIA

NEW SOUTH WALES

FRANCE

GERMANY

IRELAND

NETHERLANDS

Preamble

THIS BOOK STARTED out its life as an exercise in demonstrating that trial by jury in the twenty-first century might be, to adopt an apt phrase, no longer fit for purpose. At best it is an outstanding curiosity among civilised systems of justice in the modern world. Whatever may be the legacy of the jury system and its model of criminal trial over hundreds of years, an assessment of the case for the civilised mode of trial for serious offences, even possibly abolition for a viable system, seems ripe. It became obvious, on reading the extensive literature and having experienced the law in action, that the rival arguments for its retention or reform are nevertheless profound and not readily susceptible to rational debate. In short, each protagonist fairly resists any middle ground of compromise. Jury trial is either sacrosanct, or it is hopelessly antiquated. I have endeavoured to find a compromise. The answer depends ultimately upon the assessment of jury trial in the twenty-first century.

On the one hand, the proponents of jury trial are adamant that historically trial by jury provides a demonstrable aspect of our cherished liberties; that protection of that right against unlawful imprisonment or other serious penalty can only be preserved by any verdict of a court composed of 12 ordinary citizens (or, exceptionally, a majority of ten jurors). Trial by jury is inviolate; some of its advocates claim that it is inviolable. It is claimed that it is vital that the verdict of guilt or innocence should be uttered unreasoned. Among the remaining population, claimed to be a substantial majority, there is a growing body of opinion that seriously questions a system that opposes the legal nature of the institution of criminal justice. A number of factors that demonstrate a faulty system are accepted.

In essence, the divergence in the two strongly held views is so far apart as to be incompatible. It brooks no area of compromise. This gulf is evident in the failure of the Labour administration (from 1997 to 2010) to implement a major change in the case of serious frauds, first enacted in section 43 of the Criminal Justice Act 2003. Parliament, in that legislative act, favoured serious fraud offences being tried by a professional tribunal (with or without specialist experts), but only after a positive parliamentary motion. Subsequent attempts to activate

Parliament failed. In the Fraud Bill of 2007, a second reading of the Bill, moved by the Labour administration in the House of Lords, also failed; the Bill was accordingly dropped. And in the coalition Government in 2012, the change mooted in section 43 itself was removed. Jury trial evinces a proffered belief that reflects the English culture. From among emotional utterances, its intellectual expression is best found in the writings of the social historian, Professor EP Thompson, who wrote in 1980 in *Writing by Candlelight*, as follows:[1]

> The English common law rests upon a bargain between the Law and the People. The jury box is where people come into the court; the judge watches them and the jury watches back. A jury is the place where the bargain is struck. The jury attends in judgment, not only upon the accused, but also upon the justice and humanity of the law.

His symbiosis of the jurors and the trial judge, confirming the dual function in the forensic process, is neat. It is not hyperbolic: it is addressing the cultural context. It is a belief, devoutly sustained, in discourse or debate. Bertrand Russell once pronounced the belief as 'die hard'. Thompson's eloquence is eminently sustainable in the contemporary debate on the administration of criminal justice, such that it is only the blindfolded man who denies the provision of a perceived form of social justice. If so, the bandage can be removed by rational argument. The Enlightenment of Europe in the eighteenth century directly promoted the philosophical root of human rights. After the French Revolution of 1789–90, proposals for the formal recognition of individual human rights were put forward, culminating in the *Declaration des droits de l'homme et du citoyen* to the Assembly in August 1789 and a draft constitution. In the following year, there emerged a draft constitution for France, to which the prolific philosopher, Jeremy Bentham, in London contributed. It contained the guarantee of a citizen's right to a fair trial. This is what he wrote:

> I give it [jury trial] to those who choose to have it, in cases in which they choose to have it, and not unless they insist upon having it: looking upon it as an institution admirable in barbarous times, not fit for enlightened times, necessary as matters stand in England.

The system of jury trial, which had mainly functioned in the Anglo-Saxon world since the twelfth century, has nevertheless survived, intact, for 750 years – miraculously, some would claim. In the light of contemporary opposition to jury trial for serious offences, in the face

---

[1] (London, The Merlin Press, 1980) 108.

of substantial popularity for the ancient model, this book explains the nature and scope today of jury trial, with its minor exceptions. It explores the nature and scope of criminal trial in other parts of Europe where the model subsists only in the mixture of judiciary and lay participation. Some commentators fear that lay participants in the mixed tribunal tend to outvote the judge too often, as some in the European systems seem to do. An obvious alternative is trial by judge(s) alone, or judiciary plus expert professionals for specific offences.[2] Lord Dyson neatly posed the options. In *Justice: Continuity and Change* he notes that the Magna Carta was not the source of trial by jury, 'and only judges should sit in judgment'. Bentham described his aversion to any unprofessional court; his prescription for a codification of the law of England, years later, appeared in the ninth volume of his works, published in 1843. This book explores the alternative to jury trial, and other options for the mode of trial for specified serious offences. It is not only an argument among lawyers, but also those versed in other disciplines.

In 2003 Professor Andrew Kapardis, a professor of legal psychology, in his second edition of *Psychology and the Law*, observed that it was unlikely that we would see judges and lay persons deciding serious criminal cases in the near future. Despite the inherent contradictions of the notion of the jury, and waves of attacks by influential opponents over the years (and a few more recently), the jury has survived much public disapproval. At the beginning of the third millennium, there is a greater awareness in the global jurisdictions of lay participation in the civil and criminal law systems of Europe that implement the different models of criminal trial. As Professor Kapardis observed, different professional disciples demonstrate to a great extent that changes in economic rationalism and contemporary court management permeate the administration of criminal justice in the context of criminality in all countries.

In the present context, the jury is an erratic institution (only hyperbolically, barbarous), as revealed by legislation, restricted almost only in emergency situations. Its effects over 30 years of the Troubles in Northern Ireland increasingly disturb the proponents of the jury system, and justly so. Contemporary researchers on the subject also add to the queries over the jury. Above all, the social demands for criminal justice seem to run counter to the permanent concern for the Rule of Law, prominently so in the case of the unreasoned verdict of the jury. The absence of reasons for any such vital decision stands as a basic flaw in any system

---

[2] See Knittel and Sigler in (1972) 56 *Cambridge Law Journal* 223–28.

of justice and fairness that determines the fate of an individual charged with a breach of the criminal code. This book introduces the reader to an overview of a civilised system of criminal justice. It chronicles the origins and development of jury trial in the Anglo-Saxon world. It seeks to explain and explore the principles that lie at the heart of the mode of criminal trial. It observes the essences of different attitudes to the treatment of criminality, what the author depicts as the distinction between the professional judge and the amateur juror or lay participant, and the value of such a mixed tribunal. The book, in Chapter 3 'Reason for Reasons', expounds the direction of administrators supplying reasons for their decisions, as applicable to criminal justice. This section concludes with a discussion of the jurisprudence of the European Court of Human Rights, and its cautionary approach in *Taxquet v Belgium*.

Part of the book is devoted to the dimension of the leading European jurisdictions, prefaced by a discussion of the career judiciary and the purpose of fixing criminality – a game or a search for the truth. It underlines the abandonment of trial by jury and its replacement with the mixed tribunal in pursuance of a political will to inject a lay element into the trial process. Democracy is not an essential element in the criminal trial.

The book also notes some special features of the English system of trial by judge and jurors. The section includes a discussion of the function of the advocate and his role in the forensic arena; it notes the disappearance of forensic theatrics, after the abolition of capital punishment in 1965. It describes separately the changing role of the expert in technological and scientific issues, with the growth in scientific knowledge. The book takes a look at the appellate system in crime, from the Criminal Appeal Act 1907 to the present day. The book urges the reform of the appellate court, finding the trial decision unsatisfactory as well as unsafe. It seeks to single out any miscarriage of justice by the trial.

Other important issues are touched upon – judicial ethics and court-craft; perverse jury verdicts (the nullification of jury verdicts); the speciality of fraud offences, and the selection of models for various crimes. This section also discusses the suggested reforms of the waiver of a jury trial or the ability of the defendant to choose the mode of trial (and if so, how that might work in practice). The section ends with a discussion of the restricted exceptions to jury trial – the intimidation or inability of jurors to perform their allotted task. The experience of 30 years of judge-alone trials in Northern Ireland – the Diplock Courts – is discussed.

Finally, the book proffers its proposal for a major change in direction – involvement of the defendant in the choice of mode of trial, and the intervention (where necessary) of the expert, not merely as a witness but as an assessor to the judiciary or as a supplemental decision-maker. The choice of trial should be administered by the court administration through a committee for the management and selection of criminal trial. We should abandon the notion that one size (the jury) fits all serious criminal offences and offenders: the nature of the perceived criminality should indicate the appropriate form of criminal trial.

1

Justice and Fairness: The Basis of a Fair Trial

A T THE HEART of the public's passionate approval for the jury system – nowadays, somewhat diminishing numerically in its unadulterated adherence – there exists alongside the trial process the separation in the two systems of civil and criminal jurisdictions. If the binary systems are engaged in a uniform device of seeking justice, they were irreparably dissociated after abolition (almost) in 1934 of the jury in civil cases. (Apart from a limited application of the discarded jury in defamation trials, the civil law – in England, but not in the United States – discards the use of juries.)

If you have ever had the misfortune to be involved in a trial in the civil courts, you will have at least heard or read the reason for the judge's decision. That result comes from the process of hearing both sides of the dispute (legally represented), and the handing down of the articulated judgment (frequently reserved) which the judge gives for deciding the winner and the loser, and the costs of the case. So too, the public is alerted, because there is rightly a demand for openness of the proceedings, subject only to the extremely rare occurrence of a secret trial, to protect national security. It is unthinkable that the verdict of the court would be given without a reasoned judgment. The whole process is impregnated with a sense of awe and majesty, suitably decked out to denote the purpose of law in society, a crucial instrument of the tripartite role of democratic government. As a public institution within the legal system, professionalism is the watchword. Not so, the inscrutable verdict of the amateurs that compose the tribunal of lay persons. Why then should the result of criminal proceedings, that potentially involve the loss of liberty or of other civil rights, be so different? The harsher effect of the criminal trial needs to be explained and justified.

If you are charged with a *serious* criminal offence before a judge and jury in the criminal court or other courts composed of laymen, either alone or in participation with judges, you have no choice over the mode of trial. You will have your guilt or innocence determined by a jury uttering a monosyllabic vote. Nothing more will be offered, let alone said. Yet, subject to directions from the trial judge determining the relevant law and a summing-up of the evidence elicited in the courtroom, you will be treated with no more than the single word. But that is the English model for a fair trial before an independent and impartial court. Does it ensure that you will get a fair trial, when you are not told why the court found you guilty, or indeed innocent? Fairness is the essence of a just process.

Most, but not all (as I will explain in a later chapter of the book) democratic societies have swallowed the nascent social demands that lay participation in the judicial system can contribute materially to the trial of cases and the decisions made on evidential material that confronts the ordinary citizen in everyday existence. Indeed, they assert that it is highly desirable that there should be some lay participation in a criminal trial. The injection of a lay element into the criminal process necessitates three demotic aspects: (i) participation; (ii) representation of the lay element in the panel; and (iii) deliberation of the admitted evidence and its assessment to reach a reasoned verdict. Each of the three elements exposes problems in the mixed tribunal; each element is not without criticism that reflects the inherent question of harmonising and harnessing the principles of justiciability of the professional judge and the layman's participation in the judicial process, its most troublesome aspect being the quality of a reasoned verdict. As an academic commentator rightly observed in 2015:[1] 'the future prospect of requiring criminal courts to offer some sort of explanation for their verdicts may not be so far off on the horizon as had once been imagined'.

Every aspect of the procedure in cases of criminal trials was separately treated in principle and in practice. There was no reference to the civil system, and since the Criminal Appeal Act 1907 it has been separately administered. The twin appeal systems were administratively united in the Criminal Appeal Act 1968 under the Court of Appeal's structure. But the forensic processes for civil and criminal trials markedly differed, while some (but not all) Lords Justices of Appeal sat in both jurisdictions. That apart, the criminal law catered for appeals on law and fact to its own Division of the Court of Appeal, presided over by

---

[1] Jonathan Doak, Durham University, 'Enriching Trial Justice for Crime Victims in Common Law Systems: Lessons from Transitional Environments' (2015) 21(2) *International Review of Victimology* 139 at 146.

the Lord Chief Justice. It also allowed for appeals against the sentence imposed exclusively by the trial judge following the conviction by the jury. (In English law, the jury, strictly speaking, had no function, except indirectly by the conviction for the particular offence(s), on the question of sentencing.) If confirmation of the separateness of the criminal system were needed, the sentencing process demonstrated (and still demonstrates) such separateness, almost a juristic apartheid. The criminal practitioners form a distinct group within barristerial functions. Studies of the earlier reports of sentencing appeals disclosed the absence of any counsel for the Crown as the respondent to the appeal, although often Crown counsel did appear on the hearing of the appeal, and then only 'to assist the court'. It was accepted that any question of a penal sanction was a matter for the sentence, directing the prison administration, or other authority exercising deprivation of liberty or property, to execute the sentence of the court. Thus, effectively, the penal administration has no official standing as part of the criminal justice system. The separation of penal administration from the criminal justice process is established. The division of function in the disposal of convicted offenders is important. There is no opportunity, other than inferentially from the Crown's 'assistance' in the process of determining the appropriate sanction, for the criminal court to respond to demands from the prison administration and other penal consideration. By contrast, when the Dutch government in the recent past resolved to reduce its prison population, it gave instructions to prosecutors to lower their sights; it effectively reduced the size of the prison population, although the trend has recently been reversed. The separation of powers precludes the right of executive government from dictating penal outcomes. The example is obvious. The criminal justice system should hereafter provide an audience to the Crown about the state of the country's imprisonment.

Hitherto, there had been some doubt whether the judiciary, aside from its function in the Court of Appeal (Criminal Division), had a reviewing function over the sentencing of trial judges. The doubt was resolved by me, when unearthing, in the April 2017 issue of *Public Law*, a judicial gem in the form of a dissent by Lord Wilberforce in the House of Lords in 1971 in *Kennedy v Spratt*.[2] A positive alliance between the judicial review of civil and criminal jurisdictions was thus established, judicially. The common denominator is that both systems guarantee a fair trial before an independent and impartial judiciary. That element

---

[2] [1972] AC 83.

of independence and impartiality for trying serious criminal offences depends on the unreasoned verdict of 12 (exceptionally, it may be ten) citizens drawn at random from the lists of the electorate.

I. SENTENCING: A NON-JURY FUNCTION?

As I have noted, the jury plays no part in directly deciding the disposal of a convicted offender; jurors simply return their verdict of guilt or innocence, and the penalty imposed on the convicted defendant is exclusively a matter for the trial judge. The task for the jury is clear enough. The juror's oath demands that he or she will declare a verdict according to the evidence evinced in the courtroom, and not otherwise. He or she does so after reasonable assessment of such evidence. But what do we say about a verdict of guilt or innocence that palpably defies the terms of the oath? Does the perverse verdict prevail? If the perversity ends in a conviction, the appellate process can remedy the defect. If, however, the result is a jury acquittal, that is the end of the matter, subject only to the rare event of fresh evidence emerging in the prosecutorial investigation.[3]

The proponents of the jury system, however, argue that perverse acquittals are the prerogative of the jury and are sustainable in the eyes of the law. They constitute theoretically the appropriate nullification of the jury's verdict. Is that so? At least those commentators can properly refer to much of the jury's task effectively influencing the range of penalties in the criminal calendar.

A shining example is the case of murder. The law provides that in the case of a conviction for murder there is automatically only the sentence of life imprisonment. Some, if not most, cases of murder involve a potential alternative verdict of manslaughter which the jury may impose. If so, the judge is relieved of the mandatory sentence. He can impose a sentence of life imprisonment as a maximum, or anything less. Thus, effectively, a jury in a murder case can decide that the ultimate penalty should not be imposed, by passing a manslaughter verdict. The jury can thus properly pre-determine a penalty of less than life imprisonment. Similar, but less clear, results may arise from convictions for other offences. Much plea-bargaining that takes place is motivated by the potential of conviction for less serious offences than those initially charged.

---

[3] I have more to say about this in Chapter 14 dealing with safeguards for the unreasoned verdict.

A defence of an institution can often be a way of defending the vision that went into building it along the historical continuum. The devotion among many legal (and other) professionals for jury trial is an example of the imperfect vision. At least four factors in the last 300 years disclose the defective mode of the criminal trial; the history before the Civil War is hugely problematical. Fairness hardly emerged as a safeguard to the offender any time before the nineteenth century.

The jury system was adversarial only after the eighteenth century. As the authors of *The Trial on Trial* observed,[4] 'the turning point for the development of the modern adversarial trial', on which much pride has been expended, 'was the passing of the Treason Trials Act of 1696, permitting those charged with treason to have full access to counsel for the preparation and conduct of their defence'. Hitherto the mode of trial by one's peers had been altogether different. The impact of the 1696 reform was more subtle, with the advent of a right to a full legal defence in trials for felony, which was recognised with the passage of the Prisoners' Counsel Act 1836.

Second, it was not until 1898 that defendants were allowed to give evidence on oath, although in fact defendants routinely made statements from the dock to the court. As the US Supreme Court declared ringingly in 1970 in *Williams v Florida*,[5] the purpose of the jury trial 'is to prevent oppression by the Government', and it went on to say that

> a criminal trial is in part a search for truth. But it is also a system designed to protect 'freedom' by insuring that no one is criminally punished unless the State has first succeeded in the admittedly difficult task of convincing a jury that the defendant is guilty.

This right to the accused to go into the witness-box happily persists, but in modern times it is not often that the defendant declines to exercise that right. The attitude of putting the Crown to proof of the accused's guilt prevails in theory, if not in practice. The adversarial feature is axiomatic.

Third, the system of trial by jury was, until 1972, thoroughly undemocratic. Only property-owners qualified to sit as jurors. The only women who could qualify were spinsters and widows. Thereafter the qualification was further induced so as generally not to disqualify those who are involved in the administration of criminal justice.

Fourth, the fundamental principle of fairness for both civil and criminal jurisdictions – to ensure the equality of arms in the trial

---

[4] *The Trial on Trial* vol 3 (Oxford, Hart, 2007) at p 41.
[5] 399 US 78 (1970) at 100 and 113.

process – is vouchsafed by Article 6 of the European Convention on Human Rights, a right that was protected in England in 1966 by according the defendant the right of individual petition to the European Court. That right was further underlined in the Human Rights Act 1998 which conferred the right in domestic law.

Article 6 of the European Convention on Human Rights sets out the specific rules that relate to a defendant's rights in a criminal trial, whether or not the criminal prosecution qualifies exclusively for trial by jury. All major democracies determine the defendant's rights in some form and all have a formal presumption of innocence. Article 6 highlights the various principles requiring a conviction beyond a reasonable doubt, the presumption of innocence (evidentially, throughout the proceedings), a deep-seated approach to a conviction, and *in dubio pro reo* (if in doubt, you must decide in favour of the defendant). All these mark out the constraints on the court from deciding to condemn a defendant to a violation of his civil liberties; they all apply whatever the mode of tribunal, including a jury. The glaring omission is the reasoning which sustains the verdict. Even adjudications by lay persons in some modes of trial require some kind of rationale from the mixed tribunal. Juryless trials (infrequently used) exhibit the same treatment – a fully reasoned judgment from the court.

No global survey of evidence (as far as I am aware) about the models for criminal justice in the civilised administration of a democratic country indicates that the jury is an *essential* ingredient of a fair trial, only professional judges. Trial by jury is neither logical nor rational in the administration of a modern legal system. Judging in a trial is a professional skill; it may, however, include other considerations of a political nature which reflect media distrust (the judiciary as 'enemies of the people') by the body politic of the governing elements of its legal system. A lack of judicial independence in past centuries, as tools of the kingly rule, motivated the counterbalance of popular involvement in decision-making. Politics may reasonably influence the scope of a criminal trial in respect of more serious offences. Otherwise, however, professionalism prevails. The fair trial is the ultimate object of the European Convention on Human Rights. Article 6 so provides for the members of the Council of Europe.

About one half of the major democracies have rejected jury systems altogether; adjudications by lay persons in some form or another, however, appear, but the form they take varies a great deal. The motivation for mixed tribunals (judges and lay people) also varies.

England conspicuously favours trial by jury, but only for a fraction (about 5%) of all criminal trials. For the large remainder there is the magistracy. It is widely claimed that the vast range of criminal trials is conducted by the magistracy, a number of stipendiaries (lawyers) and appointed Justices of the Peace who are not legally qualified. Since those magistrates must undergo special training and sit for at least 26 days a year, they are recognisably selected for their magisterial role. They demonstrate a non-lawyerly expertise, but they are not amateurs in their role of decision-makers in the Magistrates' Court; they are quasi-judges.

In short, there may be cultural reasons to justify the promotion as a sign of democratic triumph, or as an aspect of the Rule of Law. If so, it emanates from neither of those constitutionalisms. As an indicator of democratic achievement it emotionally evokes the call for a jury of one's peers or of the populace, which comes stridently and resoundingly only from the United States.

If the jury is not a *necessary* qualification to the design of democratic policies, what social justification can sustain its existence, nay even its social importance? Some salutary effects may exist. Once the alleged right is modified (in essence a duty to undergo jury trial), other factors in the process of a fair trial become effective. What then is effective? The burden of this book is to examine in detail the present system and to analyse how better the mode of trial can be made. Other relevant facts about the administration of criminal justice will also be considered.

2

The Theory of Jury Function

I MPRISONMENT – THE PUTTING of people in prison – is as old as society itself. But not until the abandonment of transportation to the colonies of Australia in the 1860s was imprisonment, with its concomitant disqualifications, used as a penal sanction. Transportation was legitimised on conviction by a criminal court. Apart from the imposition of the death penalty and the mandatory sentence of life imprisonment for murder after abolition in 1965, the emerging penal system was a function of the criminal court after conviction; the jury took no part in the disposal of the offender. And so it uniquely remains the case. Most other democratic societies have variously entertained the participation of lay persons to supplement the judicial institution of the criminal court, both in decision-making over guilt or innocence and in sentencing.

Under transportation, the offender was instantly labelled as morally unfit to live in the country of his birth. If it was only a journey to a penal colony far away, it was a banishment with little or no prospect of return. Few in fact returned to their home-land after the transportation was served. The vast majority had little choice but to become emigrants to the penal settlement. As Radzinowicz and Hood, in their essay on the legacy of transportation, observed: 'Riddance from society was the ready resort as the reluctance to enforce the capital code [execution by hanging] was gaining strength'.[1] While hanging persisted for another century, it was an infrequent penalty when it was finally abolished in 1965. Thereafter, Britain learnt to consume its own smoke. The prison estate was enlarged in the latter part of the nineteenth century. But its population of convicted offenders was made up of those criminals assigned by the judiciary of the higher courts. Apart from an element of prisoners awaiting trial before the criminal courts, jurors were exclusively fact-finders of the

---

[1] L Radzinowicz and R Hood, *The Emergence of Penal Policy in Victorian and Edwardian England* (Clarendon Press, 1990) ch 14, 465 at 471.

criminal event. Sentencing became an important feature of the criminal justice system. Not so the juror.

It may seem strange that in modern penal systems, countries have accommodated variable aspects of lay participation. Legislators have produced the non-professional judge of fact within the task, jointly with the qualified judges, of determining the disposal, custodial or non-custodial, of the convicted criminal. The rationale of lay participation in the appropriate disposal of the convicted offender stemmed from the social perception that ordinary citizens should play a part in the modern system of protecting the community from further crime and for temporarily depriving the offender of his liberty. Yet, no such involvement was provided for for jurors in England and Wales.

If stripped of the duty of sentencing offenders, the juror was assumed to contribute appropriately in finding the facts of the criminal event, and doing so monosyllabically. No reason was called for, and none was given, except that which could be inferred from the verdict. I am constantly reminded of Lord Reid, an outstanding Law Lord of the 1960s and 70s. He told me once that being a judge of the law was often quite complex. But he emphasised that the task of assessing the facts was infinitely more difficult.

There are three stages in the process of a trial by jurors. The first step is to understand the nature and scope of the evidence. Nowadays that feature often involves the consideration of a vast amount of documentary material; but in many cases of criminal activity it depends on the task of assimilating the credibility and reliability of the witness, often a witness with mental or developmental disabilities. It would be foolish to argue that the attributes of the tribunal – the presiding judge and the lay capacity of the normal citizen, randomly chosen to sit with others, are well-matched. For a wide range of criminal events that are labelled as against the person and even simple property, there ought not to be a case of the two elements in the court being other than equivalent in adjudicating, if not equiparating in ability.

The second element is the assessment that should be made of the admissible evidence. (There is rightly sometimes a suspicion that individual jurors take on board knowledge acquired outside the courtroom.) But, given the assistance that the trial judge should give to the jury in his summary of the evidence, it should be assumed that there is a harnessing and assessment of fact-finding which may lack only a proper thought process.

The third element is the inviolacy of the jury deliberation and the absence of any reasons for the verdict. It is the lack of reasoning that leads me to disqualify the jury system as a mode of a criminal trial in the twenty-first century. But that apart, there is one other aspect of fact-finding that leads me to prefer trial by a judge (or judges). It is the inherent nature of human beings.

We all make decisions in our everyday life that affect the quality of other people's lives. A few of us who are trained and qualified to practise law also perform that function when acting as judges in the institutions of the judicial system. Do the two kinds of decision-maker match the other's performance? Are the acts in harmony, even when set in harness? The answers to these questions lie at the very core of the appropriate mode of tribunal to administer criminal justice. Does the civilised system of criminal justice sensibly provide for lay participation in our criminal courts? What denotes the task of the judge?

In the hierarchy of legal skills, pride of place in the English system is devoted to the exposition of legal principles, ie that manifestation of the criminal offences described in the criminal code (as yet unwritten). The judicial determination of factual issues concerning the criminal event resides in the unqualified jurors, subject to the explanation of them by the judge's summing-up in his direction to the jury. As Benjamin Cardozo states in his *Nature of the Judicial Process*,[2] 'Lawsuits are rare and catastrophic experiences for the vast majority of men, and even when the catastrophe ensues, the controversy relates most often not to the law, but to the facts'; the law is for the judge, the facts are for the jury. In deciding the facts the jury does not rely on or depend on any authority. Except for acting upon expert evidence, there is no amount of ratiocination. It relies wholly on lawless judgment.

Three features of the factual issue at trial are, first, the conflicting views of the witnesses, secondly, the formality and action of the trial process, and thirdly, the summing-up by the judge which is advisory only. Some commentators would add that the truth of the criminal event is not in issue; the observation is focused on where the burden and standard of proof lie. Thus in the English system the judge acts in an adversarial system. In the European systems the judge functions in an inquisitorial system; the truth about the criminal event is the object of the trial process. But is a juryless trial any the less adversarial? The establishment of the accused's criminality must always seem the product of conflicting views. Is that not also adversarial?

---

[2] (Yale University Press, 1921) 128–29.

The other feature of the adversarial (and probably the inquisitorial) system is the demeanour of the witness. How he or she appears and responds to the cross-examination is a vital element, a matter for the judgment on the facts. It is only at the point of deliberation and determination of guilt or innocence that the jury acts inviolately and unchallengeably. It is at this point in the process that the skill and practice of criminal justice bears upon non-factual issues of a judicial nature. As such, the fairness of the verdict is more aptly attributed to a professional lawyer than to the amateur lay person. This is usefully described as lacking justiciability in the administration of criminal trials. It is unreasoned, unaccountable and lacking in transparency. Inscrutability is injustice.

3

Reason for Reasons

A CIVILISING INFLUENCE on the decision-making of central and local government is the administrator's explanation for the unreasoned verdict (act or omission) of the administrative decision touching on some aspect of the citizen's life. Whether, however, there has developed an enforceable duty to give reasons in administrative law is questionable if evolutionary. By now (2018) there is a marked shift away from the general rule in administrative justice of not requiring a reasoned verdict towards a general rule to give reasons unless otherwise indicated by the legislative authority, or if there is some other powerful justification for their absence. Elias LJ concluded in *Oakley v South Cambridgeshire District Council*, that[1]

> it may be more accurate to say that the common law is moving to the position whilst there is no universal obligation to give reasons in all circumstances, in general they should be given unless there is a proper justification for not doing so …

This is an emphatic shift from the idea expressed in *R v HEFC, ex p Institute of Dental Surgery*,[2] per Sedley LJ, that apparently aberrant decisions would displace the general rule that there is no universal obligation to give reasons in all circumstances; they should be given unless there is a proper justification for not doing so. In short, the rule of generality is now reversed.

In the absence of a specific statutory requirement to give reasons for administrative decisions, no general duty exists, but in *R v Secretary of State for the Home Department, ex p Doody*,[3] the House of Lords confirmed that there is no general duty for administrative decisions. That definite ruling was somewhat qualified by Lord Mustill's statement in

---

[1] *Oakley v South Cambridgeshire District Council* [2017] EWCA Civ 71, [2017] 1 WLR 3765.
[2] *R v HEFC, ex p Institute of Dental Surgery* [1994] 1 WLR 242.
[3] *R v Secretary of State for the Home Department, ex p Doody* [1994] 1 AC 531.

his judgment in *Doody* that 'nevertheless it is broadly beyond question, that such a duty may in appropriate circumstances be applied'. The House of Lords based its decision on the requirements of fairness. Lord Mustill endorsed the analysis of the factors material to the implication of such a duty. He said that the decision conferred a duty where there was a presumption that it would be exercised in a manner which is fair in all the circumstances. Fairness required that reasons be given. The sufficiency of the reasons will depend on the nature of the subject-matter of the administrative decision – if in public law, why not criminal justice?

All commentators regard the provision of reasoned decisions as an essential component of fair procedure. Official bodies have demonstrated a similar enthusiasm. Prompted by the academic interest in the extended subject by Genevra Richardson, in 'The Duty to Give Reasons: Potential and Practice',[4] I took up the theme of fairness, when acting as a Deputy High Court judge in *R v London Borough of Lambeth, ex p Walters*,[5] a judicial review case on the homelessness legislation of 1985. Adopting the approach of Lord Mustill in *Doody* to ask the question: 'is the refusal to give reasons fair?', I considered that it was not fair. I held that it was unfair of Lambeth Borough Council not to ensure that the applicant for accommodation by an unintentionally homeless person had every opportunity of seeing and assessing the strength of medical evidence about her four-year-old son who suffered from spina bifida; it was also unfair of the local authority to have proceeded to determine which of the conflicting medical evidence should prevail. I held that there was a general duty to give reasons whenever the statutorily impregnated social administrative process was infused with a concept of fair treatment for those directly affected. Criminal justice is inherently the receptacle for fairness and rationality.

While academic comment was not entirely supportive, it was explicable on the lack or inadequacy of reasons in coming to a reasonable decision. If reasonable, *cadit questio*, reasoning would not assist the applicant. Mr NR Campbell, a lecturer in law at Nottingham University, wrote[6] that my assertion that fairness demanded such a process 'may be premature'; at that time the decision under challenge would be reviewed if there was a particular need for explanation. Maybe fairness qualified for explanation.

---

[4] (1986) *PL* 437–69. Professor Richardson was then a lecturer in law at the University of East Anglia, later Professor of Law at the University of London.
[5] *R v London Borough of Lambeth, ex p Walters* [1994] 26 HLR 170.
[6] (1994) *PL* 184–90.

No appeal from my reasoned decision on judicial review took place. And I am unaware that, 25 years later, it stands as an authority. But, since the requirement under section 17(3) of the Inquiries Act 2005 is that the proceedings of a public inquiry should be conducted by a Commissioner of Inquiry, acting on behalf of a ministerial decision, fairness attains a status that calls for reasoned decisions. Does it inevitably follow?

Trial by jury – not a part of public administration, but a public institution under human rights legislation – must be counted as an exception. If not required to deliver a verdict for its reason, at least the proponents of it are keen to insist that reasons are implied from among the evidence adduced publicly and further enunciated by an adequate summing-up by the trial judge.

If the principle of fairness is limited to equality of treatment to the contestants in a dispute, there is something to be said for taking account of the extent of any liability of the administrator. The parties in dispute may well understand the decision and adjudge its reasonableness. Reasonableness of the decision contributes to the openness and fairness of that decision, and the administrative process that is effected in the decision-making. Above all, the standard of decision-making and consistency of decisions provides the party with a foundation for consideration of the possibility of taking a case to the High Court for judicial review, limited as it is to ensuring legality without an appeal. In summary, the benefits commonly attributed by official bodies to the giving of reasons are: fairness or satisfaction to the parties; the improvements in decision-making, and the facilitation of appeals, arbitrarily within the system of public administration. At a glance, those arguments reflect the full range of the analyses of the administrative process; all those considerations encompass the influence of the Rule of Law in its various guises. But are they adequate to meet the insistence on greater transparency in decision-making and the accountability to the public of good government? The nascent growth of fairness, not only to the instant parties but also to the desirability of extended public accounts of administrative cases, is now demanding further consideration of fairness.

A third factor in our law has always been acknowledged. It is the quality of reasoning. To judge the validity and legitimacy of any verdict is best maintained by the thought process that sustains the verdict. Certainty of treatment and the clarity of expressed thought are vital components in sound and safe decision-making. It is also clarity of reasoning that persuades the observer that standards are met, in particular that preconditions and prejudices (in addition to bias) are effectively controlled by the decision-maker. In short, the administrative process demands a dignified response. Reasons do that much. In *Re Poyser and Mills' Arbitration*,[7] Megaw J described the process well: 'a person's property and other reasons might have been gravely affected by a decision of some official, the decision might have been perfectly right, but the person against whom it was made was left with the real grievance that he was not told why the decision has been made'. The ability of reasons to improve the quality of decision-making has often been emphasised, if only because it ensures that the decision-maker does not make a mistake, does not omit anything relevant to the decision and arrives at a reasonable conclusion.

On 2 October 2000 the Human Rights Act 1998 came into force, enacting into UK law the European Convention on Human Rights. Article 6 of the Convention provides that everyone is entitled to a fair and public hearing before an independent and impartial tribunal established by law. The Convention does not define the notion of a 'fair trial'.[8] The rights specified in Article 6(2) (the presumption of innocence) and Article 6(3) (the list of minimum standards) are not exhaustive of the content of a fair trial in Article 6(1). A trial may still not conform to the general standard of a fair trial, even if the minimum rights guaranteed have been fully respected. The question, therefore, whether the trial does conform to Article 6 will not be decided on the basis of an isolated consideration of one particular incident. It is on an evaluation of the entire criminal process, from arrest to verdict, that the answer must be given to the question whether there has been a fair trial.

One of the several, more concrete rights which have been enunciated is the right to know the grounds on which a court decision is based. In *Van de Hurk v The Netherlands*[9] the court held that:

> Article 6(1) obliges courts to give reasons for their decisions, but cannot be understood as requiring a detailed answer for every argument. Nor is the European Court called upon to examine whether arguments are adequately met.

The extent of the objective to give reasons may also vary according to the nature of the decision and the circumstances of each case.[10] How does the verdict uttered by the foreman of the jury in answer to the

---

[7] *Re Poyser and Mills' Arbitration* [1964] 2 QB 467, 478.
[8] *Nielsen v Denmark* (1989) 11 EHRR 175 para 52.
[9] *Van de Hurk v The Netherlands* (1994) 18 EHRR 481 para 61.
[10] *Ruiz Torija v Spain* (1995) 19 EHRR 553; *Hiro Balani v Spain* (1995) 19 EHRR 566; see also *Georgiadis v Greece* (29 May 1997) RJD 1997 III No 38: 24 EHRR 606 (failure to give sufficiently detailed reasons).

court's question, 'guilty or not guilty' (or, alternatively in Scotland, 'not proven') measure up to the standard of a fair trial? Hitherto, the Court of Appeal has discouraged the practice of juries doing anything more than answering the question: 'Do you find the accused guilty or not guilty?'

The Court of Appeal hinted, albeit obliquely, how the requirement of Article 6 to give reasons would apply in a civil case. In *Flannery v Halifax Estate Agencies Ltd*,[11] Lord Justice Henry, in delivering the judgment of the court, said:

> The duty [of a judge to give reasons for his decision] is a function of due process, and therefore of justice. Its rationale has two principal aspects. The first is that fairness surely requires that the parties – especially the losing party – should be left in no doubt why they have won or lost. This is especially so, since without reasons the losing party will not know ... whether the court has misdirected itself, and thus whether he may have an available appeal on the substance of the case. The second is that a requirement to give reasons concentrates the mind. If it is fulfilled, the resulting decision is much more likely to be soundly based on the evidence than if it is not.

Where does this leave due process and fairness in trial by jury? In *R v Boreman*,[12] the Court of Appeal (Criminal Division) said that, 'theoretically', there were four possible conclusions on the facts of that case which could have led the jury to its verdict of guilty. The Court of Appeal eliminated two of these possibilities, on the ground that 'no juror could properly have reached [them]'. The Court could not know that the jury had not followed a possible route which the judges considered improper – it is by no means unknown for a jury to reach a conclusion by an inadmissible route, though we rarely find out about it. And, in any event, that left two possibilities. There is nothing unusual about this. It must be the case in many, if not most jury trials.

In *Flannery* the Court ordered a new trial, because the judge had not given any reasons for his preference of the expert evidence called by the plaintiff to that called by the defendant. On the footing that, on a matter involving something in the nature of an intellectual exchange, with reasons and analysis advanced on either side, the judge must deal with the issues canvassed before him and explain why he preferred the one rather than the other. The Court further stated that reasons were particularly necessary in litigation involving expert evidence, 'but it is not necessarily limited to such cases'.[13]

[11] *Flannery v Halifax Estate Agencies Ltd* [2000] 1 WLR 377.
[12] *R v Boreman* [2000] 1 All ER 307.
[13] [2000] 1 WLR 377 at 382B.

In criminal trials it often happens that the jury has to decide between the differing views of expert witnesses; the accused has no idea why the jury preferred the one to the other. The case of Sally Clark[14] is an exemplification of the problem facing a jury that has heard conflicting evidence of experts – 14 of them in that case. Is that 'due process' and 'justice' in the criminal court when it would not be so in the civil court? In *Carr*,[15] Lord Bingham CJ, while not wishing to encourage the exchanges of paper which characterise civil proceedings, thought it 'anomalous and wrong that a case against a defendant should be spelled out with less particularity when he stands in the dock accused of murder than when he resists a claim for compensation'. It would be difficult to quarrel with that proposition. Is the position regarding reasons, however, any less 'anomalous and wrong'?

The courts have often said that juries cannot be expected to give coherent reasons for their decisions, and regularly do not do so. There could be no better illustration of the enormity of the task they might face in doing so. The trial judge in *Boreman* found it necessary to instruct the jury in the law relating to murder, causation, self-defence, provocation, the effect of intoxication on the specific intent in murder, and the 'all-important matter of joint enterprise', to say nothing of standard directions on the burden and the standard of proof – at least half a term's course for an undergraduate studying criminal law. In addition, the judge ought to have directed them as to the need for unanimity on the basis of each defendant's guilt. The judge would deal only with those aspects of the law which were relevant to the present case; but this was a formidable task for him, and much more so for the jury. And what about the assessment and evaluation of the facts, on which the judge was bound in his summing-up to assist the jury? The jury could never reasonably have been expected to give coherent reasons for its decision on each of these matters. Indeed, they would probably not be able to produce composite reasons this side of Doomsday. Could the judge, like his French counterpart, retire with the jury to help compose reasons? If Justices' clerks are not allowed to retire with their Justices, other than to tell them about the relevant law, there is a recognition that the mix of decision-makers would be unacceptable. Yet we do have a kind of mix, the summing-up of the judge purporting to assist, even influence the jurors.

But if the giving of reasons is an essential feature of due process and of justice, and if it is impracticable to require juries to give reasons,

---

[14] *R v Sally Clark* [2003] EWCA Crim 1020, [2003] 2 FCR 447.
[15] *R v Carr* [2000] Crim LR 193.

where does that leave the jury system in an English trial, now dressed up in European garb?

Jury trial in England and Wales, as I have already noted, is in fact trial by judge and jury. The former has the duty to direct the jury on the law and to sum up the relevant facts. Judge and jury, in performing their discrete functions, have a symbiotic relationship, even if symbiosis stops short of direct communication in the deliberative process. The most the jury can do is to return to court and ask for further directions on the law and guidance on relevant factual issues. But we have no idea about the chemistry of that relationship. Juries are presumed to do what they are told is the law. But there is evidence, almost entirely anecdotal, that juries will occasionally, even perversely, defy the judge who indicates a conviction, and will acquit. Conversely, a judge who leans towards an acquittal will sometimes be rebuffed by a convicting jury. Given the opacity of the problem, what will the courts say about jury trial and the right to a fair trial which involves essentially a reasoned verdict of the decision-maker?

A possible approach will be to say that the complementary role of the judge and jury adequately satisfies the requirement of the reasoned decision. Assuming that the jury loyally follows the judge's directions on the law, and is fully apprised of all the relevant facts, the standard of a fair trial would be adequately met. But it will mean that trial judges will have to tailor their recitation of the facts in a way that supplies, by a process of forensic interaction, the requirement of reasons. It will mean that the Court of Appeal (Criminal Division) will have to be more insistent on a high quality summing-up. No latitude, along the lines that the jury will have listened carefully to all the evidence without careful exposition of the relevant evidence, will be permitted, although there are few judicial advocates for abolishing the summing-up of the facts to the jury. An additional requirement will be for the judge at the conclusion of the summing-up to formulate specific questions to which the jury will be required to provide yes or no answers. Some judges already do provide short questionnaires. Directions on the law should likewise invariably be reduced to writing.

The future survival of the jury system is clearly under threat from the new legal order of the Human Rights Act 1998 and the necessity to provide reasons as an essential ingredient of a fair trial. What, one wonders, would be the position in the United States, where juries decide the guilt or innocence of accused persons without any assistance from the Bench on the facts to be determined? It is an intriguing question that a foreigner – at least this one – dares not seek to answer. But the spate of wrongful convictions, which led to the Governors of Illinois and Maryland calling a moratorium on the death penalty, at least demands an explanation of the criminal convictions in capital cases. More elaborate evidential safeguards and a sophisticated process of instructing juries may emerge for reform, whatever may be the impact on the death penalty.

It is far from obvious that the English will turn to the alternative of trial by judge alone, even if public opinion were to be impressed by the experience of the Diplock Courts. (It is curious how the English legal profession appears to refuse even to acknowledge the existence of terrorist trials in Northern Ireland, let alone their success in achieving justice.) No mini-Parliament there. Jury trial is, for good or ill, rooted in the cultural tradition of the English. Contemporary debates on the mode of trial, moreover, do not encourage any such movement towards a professionalist system. Even minor attempts to restrict the system of jury trial for all indictable crimes are surprisingly frustrated in the legislative process.

In 1986 a Committee on Fraud Trials recommended that for serious fraud cases, there should be trial by judge and two expert assessors. The Committee's recommendation of a Fraud Trials Tribunal was not suggested as an option, but as a replacement to the jury trial. The Government of the day, under considerable pressure from the Criminal Bar, rejected the proposal. But might not trial by professionals be a choice for some accused persons? Again, such a proposal has been rejected, so far. It is a fact that every day of the week, in the Chancery Division of the High Court, victims of financial fraud are suing the perpetrators of the fraud. A single Chancery judge tries the case in a civil jurisdiction, to the assumed satisfaction of the litigants in contrast to the vagaries of the criminal process. The creation of an administrative penalty for market abuse, backed up by an appellate tribunal under the Financial Services and Markets Act 2000,[16] is a sign of the times in a shift away from the criminal jurisdiction to an administrative process within the civil, regulatory system.

The jury is the highpoint, the apotheosis of amateurism,[17] potentially a recipe for incompetence and unbridled bias. The mood of civilised systems of criminal justice increasingly demands professionalism from those operating the trial process. I do not mean to be contemptuous of

---

[16] See Parts VIII and IX.
[17] See Blom-Cooper, *Power of Persuasion* (Hart Publishing, 2015), chapter 9.

the amateur's ability to judge human conduct, only the task of evaluating evidence in the courtroom, which is a job for professionals, not for occasional amateurs. We should be able to trust those trained to be judges. Jerome Frank, in his *Courts on Trial*,[18] said: 'It is, I think, wiser to trust a competent, honest judge, with a trained intuition, than twelve inexperienced laymen'. The cases brought to the criminal courts often nowadays invite a sophisticated approach to the undertaking and appreciation of recondite expert evidence, particularly on scientific and technical issues. Writing in 1859, James Fitzjames Stephen said:

> Few spectacles, it may be said, can be more absurd and incongruous than that of a jury composed of twelve persons who, without any previous scientific knowledge or training, are suddenly called upon to adjudicate in controversies in which the most eminent scientific men flatly contradict each other's assertions. How, it might be asked, can ordinary tradesmen and farmers, who have never been accustomed to give sustained attention to any subject whatever for an hour together, be expected to weigh evidence, the delivery of which occupies many days and which bears upon subjects which can only be described in language altogether new and foreign to their understanding?[19]

And he concluded:

> We ought to take seriously that when scientific questions are involved in a criminal trial, the verdicts upon which courts of justice pronounce judgment should represent the settled opinions of men who have made a special study, and not the loose impressions of unscientific jurors.[20]

Scientific evidence has tended to become more complex and forensically controversial. Evaluation of often complex financial transactions, transparency in the reasoning process of the decision-makers and the demand for a full appellate system, in which the court can freely overturn the trial court's verdict, quite apart from the escalating cost to the public purse, all dictate expertise and experience of qualified judges to try the most serious criminal cases. That approach to a modern criminal justice system will tend to inform the interpreters of Article 6.

And change to trial by judge without jury, if it comes at all, will inevitably be slow and initially minimal in its advent. The British are likely for years ahead to remain wedded to the institution, but the

---

[18] (1950) at 252.
[19] James Fitzjames Stephen, *Trial by Jury and the Evidence of Experts* (London Papers of the Juridical Society, 1858–1863) vol 1, Paper XIV, at 236.
[20] ibid.

cornerstone of jury trial is being gradually chipped away. The masonry is gradually losing its angularity, to the point where the new surface will uncover optional modes of criminal trial. We need to start educating the British public that the gradual dismantling, or even ultimate disappearance of its cherished institution will not be disastrous. It will in fact bring clarity and purpose to a civilised process of ensuring justice to both prosecutor and prosecuted. True justice must be even-handed.

Logic and rationality argue forcibly against the jury as the exclusive decision-maker for less than one per cent of all prosecuted crimes. But the assumed public confidence in the system will be likely to persuade, to the point of retention of the jury system in the foreseeable future. One factor that lies behind the oft-repeated preference for lay adjudication over trial by judge alone (or perhaps three judges) is the public trust in and estimation of the jury. There is little, if any, doubt that our judges in the Crown Court are appointed on a meritocratic basis, and significantly not popularly elected as in the State jurisdictions of the USA, and are thus 'independent and impartial', free from the taint of political aspirations, at least since the late 1950s. Nevertheless, there is a belief among the public that judges appointed under the English legal system are remote from the lives of ordinary citizens and hence are handicapped at assessing the conduct of witnesses and accused persons. That stands in sharp contrast to the public's confidence in judges heading public inquiries, above all other professional and non-professional tribunals. And will not the Judicial Appointments Commission erase the image of judicial remoteness from the lives of ordinary citizens?

Since government has no specific interest in the prosecution of crime, other than to bring offenders to justice on behalf of victims and society generally, the judge cannot properly be seen as favouring the Crown rather than the accused in the dock. There is no basis for imputing perceived bias, one way or another. Individual prejudice and preconception is readily avoidable by the precepts of judiciality. It may be that where the offence charged is one of the crimes against the State (eg the Official Secrets Act), civil liberties might at least dictate a choice of trial by judge alone or by a jury of 12 lay persons. That apart, we should begin to modify the system of jury trial, at least by developing the waiver, giving a choice to the accused of the mode of his or her trial. Another modification should be the change to trial by special tribunal for serious fraud cases for reasons of economy of resources and time, as well as to remove the strain on jurors; they will at least serve to demonstrate the validity of professionalism in criminal justice. And if the police evidence of intimidation and harassment of jurors and witnesses is valid, is not the example of the Diplock Courts sufficient to justify trial by judge alone?

Trial by judge alone, in restricted classes of case, may establish whether the lay element in the judge/jury system does provide added value to criminal justice. If so, there may be room, particularly in complex fraud cases, for a tribunal composed of judge and specialist assessors as the joint decision-makers. Other modes of trial, compliant with Article 6 of the ECHR, might also merit consideration.

These modifications of trial by judge and jury for indictable offences are modest inroads to the system. Far from the introduction of a 'two-tier', discriminatory procedure, the comparison might be highly informative and evocative, even in the absence of any social research into the inner (secretive) workings of juries; at least judge-alone trials cannot be excluded from research.

The growing importance of the giving of reasons for any decision of a tribunal or administrator is evident from modern European legislation. Its European origin lies in Article 253 of the Rome Treaty, and has achieved elaboration in Article 296 of the Treaty dealing with the functioning of the European Union. The Article reads as follows:

> Where the Treaties do not specify the type of act to be adopted, the institutions shall select it on a case-by-case basis, in compliance with the applicable procedures and with the principle of proportionality.

> Legal acts shall state the reasons on which they are based and shall refer to any proposals, initiatives, recommendations, requests or opinions required by the Treaties.

> When considering draft legislative acts, the European Parliament and the Council shall refrain from adopting acts not provided for by the relevant legislative procedure in the area in question.

It can hardly be gainsaid that the verdict of the jury about the guilt or innocence of a defendant is, intrinsically, of prime significance, and not to be doubted.

4

European Dimensions

A NY COMPARISON BETWEEN the modes of criminal trial prescribed in western Europe would involve going further than a book, such as this one, which seeks only to understand the nature of unreasoned verdicts in jury trial in England. To work out fully the various comparable systems, it would be necessary to superimpose a detailed study of the differences which exist in the systems of legal procedure and substantive law. It would be pitchforking the reader into a very bulky treatise. That is not my purpose. If the reader is subjected only to a very limited glance at various modes of criminal trial, it is nevertheless helpful to isolate three fundamental issues in establishing a civilised system of criminal justice. An examination of the philosophical principles may thus serve to explain the different atmospheres and approaches to the judicial conduct of a fair trial.

The first quality that is asked for in a judicature, whether in civil or criminal trial, is that it should be *independent*, that is to say that it is not swayed by governmental influence, nor by a party to the proceedings or by outside pressures exerted through the government as medium. To secure this, the judge is made practically irremovable in modern democracies; any offences regarding irremovability are restricted to details of no material consequence. There remains the question of promotion. The judge in western Europe, who is a member of a minutely graduated hierarchy, inevitably thinks of his promotion up through the career system, and he will look for his advancement to the Ministry of Justice as the governing body, according to varieties of parliamentary constitution, what the American poet Walt Whitman called the 'never-ending audacity of elected persons'. In the English tradition, the danger was typically avoided, rather more by chance than by design. Since the present system of establishing a Judicial Appointments Committee in England, the prospect of promotion has been eliminated, even if hitherto officially unrecognised. Even if the promotional urge is personally felt, any influence of government has been internally erased. Political activity plays no part in the appointment of judges, at least for the last 40 years.

Hitherto, political activists were clearly advantaged by Lord Chancellors of the past.

A second requirement is that a judge should act impartially, that is not venal. The judicial element is irrelevant. The argument relies on the higher earnings of a successful career as an advocate in the courtroom while aspiring to the status of judgeship. So long as the criminal judiciary is drawn at all levels from among those who experienced criminal trials as representatives of clients. Judges on the continent of Europe are less well-paid than their counterparts in England, because they are instantly on the bottom rung of the ladder of a judicial hierarchy in a career profession, starting from the age of 26, and university graduated. While they are recruited differently, there is no evidence that either system produces anything but a total commitment to independence and impartiality. Impartiality springs from the nature of umpiring disputes even-handedly, in a specialised form of justiciability (a polite word for court-craft).

A third quality is that a judge should be highly skilled, comprising aptitude, experience and learning. The establishment of a Judicial Appointments Commission satisfies the requirement that merit is the main, if not the sole, criterion. The argument over the quality of selection surrounds the need for diversity between the sexes, whereby in practice the outcome produces a minority of women judges. Less controversially, much more the consequence of ethnic minorities within the practitioners available is still actively deficient. By contrast, other systems which draw their candidates from among those entering the judicial service from university and judicial colleges present no such worry. The potential judges are self-selected by their choice of career and their qualifications as candidates.

The fact is that the task of the European judge differs widely from that of English judges, because they have such a differently expressed law to interpret. Interpretation of the law is derived from Codes, and the English from case-law. But since the common law is now overwhelmingly replaced by statute, this is more theory than practice. But the failure in England to codify the criminal law, despite efforts by the Law Commission to attract government support to undergo the task, remains a matter of adverse comment within the profession.

The distinction underlying the difference between the mode of recruiting and training judges and those prevailing in western Europe is pervasive. The creation of a Judicial Studies Board, in the latter part of the twentieth century in England, acknowledged the gap but only marginally touched on the training of judges. For reasons of academic qualifications for entry into the hierarchy of the judging system, the European judge is better equipped to handle the administration of the courtroom, particularly the criminal code. The judge in England is, on the face of academic learning and justiciability in the courtroom, less proficient in mastering the transition from the Bar to the Bench, although the transition is still achievable. Academicism among English lawyers (which dates from an ancient quarrel between the old universities and the remoteness of the control of admission to the profession via the Inns of Court) is only a relic of the past in legal education divided between the law teacher in the universities and the professional, focused heavily on the metropolis of London. It is true that by the last quarter of the nineteenth century, the leading academics like Maitland, Pollock and Dicey provided elegantly the intellectual content of the law in action. The gap began to close; by the twenty-first century, the difference was historical fact, which had lost most of its meaning. The change among the judiciary to engage publicly in issues of legal policy did much to bring the two together in harmony, but not in harness.

While advocacy (largely untutored outside the courtroom) is not a good preparation for judgeship, it is much less certain that a practice almost exclusively in the Crown Courts dealing with serious criminal offences is any kind of qualification for criminal judgeship. The aspect of the criminal jurisdiction that focuses on the sentencing of offenders is of particular concern. A close knowledge of the penal system and the practical working effect of the vast array of sentences which the legislature indulges in has been a major factor in the growth of the prison population, marked by an increase in the length of prison sentences passed by an uninformed (but not ill-informed) judiciary. The only area that needs attention is that the English judge, unlike his European counterpart who understands a court's role in the penal system, should display some scientific grounding in psychology and a current familiarity with the progress of penological ideas and penal institutions. Those criminal judges who have, since 1967, served as members of the Parole Board and adapted their skills to the problem of sentencing have been shown to be the better criminal judges in assessing the risks of discharge from custody. Admirable at presiding over and conducting jury trials in assisting jurors to their verdicts by competent summings-up, on the task of passing sentences they apply a mechanistic practice and often affect social conduct (perverse acquittals by the jury are an example). Britain has the highest prison population in western Europe (83,000 persons in 2018) due in part to the failure of the courts to curtail the punitive elements in society. Criminologists may rightly complain that their promptings for a better-informed sentencing system have gone unheeded. Only the entrance of the Sentencing Council, directed exclusively to ensure consistency among sentences, has mitigated the effect of a thoroughly distorted penal system. A welcome attitude of positive rehabilitation is beginning to shift the focus of control to the community.

If, in administering different modes of criminal trial, the various systems seem generally to convey the like desire to buttress a fair trial, there is one aspect of the binary systems that portrays a fundamental approach towards a quality of criminal justice. Every prosecutor pursues a criminal conviction according to a high standard of proof of the evidential material. The assumption is that the material must attain a standard that excludes a question of reasonable doubt, more recently a degree of confidence that sustains a conviction. Anything less deserves an acquittal of the criminal charge. It is a legal acquittal, effectively declaring only that there is a suspicion of complicity in the criminal conduct. The presumption of innocence, declared positively in Article 6 of the European Convention on Human Rights, is purely evidential. On conviction or acquittal by the trial process, the presumption is effectively displaced. It has no other effect, legally or otherwise. To reach a verdict on the relevant evidence attracts quite different approaches that may, only infrequently, result in diametrically different verdicts.

I. THE GOAL OF THE TRIAL PROCESS

To any ordinary citizen in the Anglo-Saxon world, a criminal trial is a game played by the two contestants of prosecutor and accused. The accused merely has to wait for the prosecutor to prove the case for a conviction; he or she need do nothing more than defeat the prosecutor's evidence without any assistance in that process. Until 1898, when the defendant was accorded the right to give evidence, the accused could not defend himself. Even then, it became the practice for a defendant to remain silent. But now, although the defendant still seeks to await the case against him, it is rare for an accused to stay out of the witness box. In a few cases, he deigns to state his case, if calculated that he has fully answered the questions put to him in the course of the investigation.[1] If he does want to say his part, he is usually the first witness to give

---

[1] See the discussion in chapter 16 below.

evidence, that is if the trial judge concludes that at the end of the prosecution's case there is a case to answer. (In Europe the accused, in the face of the dossier prepared by the investigating magistrate – at the judge's instruction – is invariably the first witness to be called to give evidence.) He is the primary actor in the criminal event.

If it is axiomatic that everyone charged with a criminal offence is guaranteed a fair trial before an impartial and independent tribunal, it is a good deal less certain whether the liability for crime can be appropriately attributed in arriving at a fair verdict of guilt or innocence. It is altogether one thing to make sure that the proceedings of a criminal trial are conducted fairly; an appellate system to review the trial process should ensure that the trial was fair. But it is altogether another matter whether the verdict of the court is fairly arrived at. A fair verdict depends on issues raised in the court of trial. First, there must be evidence that substantiates the conviction; availability of the factors that constitute the event must be accessible to the court, which will depend on the quality of the investigating agent (the police) and the competence (or better) of the prosecuting authority's advocacy; equally, there must exist the ability of the defendant to ward off the high quality of the evidence. Equality of arms is an essential ingredient. Judicial review can take care of any abuse of the criminal process. Second, there is the quality of the evidence. Does the system provide the opportunity to test the credibility and reliability of the witness sufficiently to establish a true verdict? Third, what is the standard of proof? Does a civilised system of criminal justice demand a degree of proof more exacting than that which one would apply in the course of normal decision-making? Is a reasonable doubt about proof of guilt too high? If so, is something less than that high standard sufficient to enter a half-way verdict of legal as opposed to factual guilt? (A separate chapter is called for, setting out the scope of innocence of criminality and its relationship to the civil liability in tort or delict.)

On the question of relevant evidence, testimony of the criminal event is all-important. Absent direct evidence of the commission of the crime, there is the fall-back on the undoubted value of circumstantial evidence. Do the circumstances leading up to and surrounding the criminal event provide a conclusive finding that there is no explanation other than the commission of the crime? Here, there is a vital element in the development of technological evidence. The advent of deoxyribonucleic acid (DNA) – the hereditary material present in the cells of all human beings – has now (as with other technological advances) impacted on the criminal law, in marked contrast to the criminal trial of the past.

Professional audiences are alive to this shift in the volume of evidence, enhanced largely due to the explosion of relevant scholarship and by investigative agencies in unmasking the culprit. The public inquiry into the Litvinenko case in 2016 is a prime instance of modern forensic development, the tracing of the deadly poison across the continent of Europe.

Judge Jerome Frank (together with his daughter Barbara), a federal Court of Appeal judge in the USA, wrote in 1957 about the jury system, observing that errors of perception and memory of eye-witnesses and victims are not uncommon. They may misinterpret, misunderstand, misremember or even give falsified testimony at trial, and hold 'undetected prejudices' that lead them to perverse verdicts. Overall, the system of trial by jury is what I describe in *Power of Persuasion* as the 'apotheosis of amateurism'. A criminal trial requires, even demands, the skills of professionally trained practitioners in a literate society. But that is not the only factor that differentiates the two methods of criminal trial that persist in western Europe. Back in the middle of the twentieth century, Professor RCK Ensor in *Courts and Judges* neatly described the two trial systems – the first is the trial staged as a fight or competition between lawyers, in combat over the goal of guilt beyond a reasonable doubt (or certainty of conviction); the jury remains the arbiter in an unarticulated verdict that is largely unappealable. The rival system is less disputatious. It aims to elicit the truth. The trial is not a game, but an exercise in eliciting the true facts of the case; they may not always coincide.

The sense of gamesmanship, however, has been substantially eroded by rules of criminal procedure. The first inroad into the principle of a game came in the Criminal Justice Act 1967 when the defendant became obliged to reveal the nature of any alibi he might wish to contest in his trial. Thereafter, several statutory provisions called upon the accused to reveal the nature of any defence and provisions for the disclosure before trial of relevant material. Case-management by the prospective trial judge has increasingly shifted the burden of evidence a long way onto the defence. A right to silence remains in theory, although there are exceptions to the rule that the defendant has no obligation to respond to any interrogation by the police. The English system has now accepted that the adversarial process of the trial acknowledges the inquisitorial system in Europe that seeks to establish the truth about the circumstances surrounding the commission of the crime. Is it not high time that the English system adopts an approach, that impressionistically jurors apply, of a trial to reveal the truth about the accused's complicity?

Fairness, after all, is as much a pre-requisite of a true verdict as it is in an even-handed game or adversarial encounter. Fairness is the guarantee of an equality of arms at every stage of the criminal prosecution, and not just apportioned piecemeal to the rival disputants.

Any disparity between the various systems of criminal trial has been further eroded by modern developments in forensic science, in two matters of relevant evidence. Many miscarriages of justice occurred as a result of false confessions or admissions by an accused. They had often been excluded from the trial because they had been improperly obtained in the course of police interrogation. The Police and Criminal Evidence Act 1984 – one of the most significant pieces of legislation – largely cured the defect of improper statements induced by police investigations. The requirement to record any statement effectively avoided any impossible confession.

II. LAY PARTICIPATION

Lay participation in criminal trials is widely imported into the European system. But it is unknown today in the Dutch system, apart from a short period in the early nineteenth century when the Netherlands became part of France under the Napoleonic regime. As from 1 March 1811 the Netherlands became part of the French Empire; legislation required two different forms of administration of justice. The first was trial by jury in criminal cases; the second was the administration of justice by laymen in commercial courts. The Dutch legal system had a third form of participation by laymen, the mixed administration of justice which in this variant saw laymen administering justice in cooperation with professional judges. After Napoleon's defeat at Waterloo, juries were abolished in the Netherlands in December 1813, the main reason being an aversion by the judges to juries; they represented the symbol of public suspicion against the judges. The assumption was thought to be unwarranted by a judiciary which at that time seemed to be trustworthy. The debate, however, persisted. By the end of the nineteenth century, the industrial revolution had so immeasurably progressed that, whatever the status of the judiciary, they were being criticised for their excessive formalism and being out of touch with social reality. The debate persisted; the abolition of juries did not end the discussion, an attitude fed by the lack of openness in the justice system. It was considered that enabling the public to take part in the legal system was the answer. But it did not end the debate. In 1929 a professor in law at Amsterdam weighed up the advantages and disadvantages; he concluded for no change, although the constitution was silent on whether juries could be brought back, even if different in form from the French mode. Discussion showed that lay participation was inspired by events in Germany. But the issue was linked with hostility to lay involvement in civil cases, including commercial disputes, and lay participation in administrative law. A prominent Amsterdam lawyer, advising the public authorities, was JA Levy. Levy had no faith in jury trials. As Professor Corjo Jansen explains in his article, 'The Participation of Laymen in the Dutch Judiciary (1811–2011)',[2] Levy's motto in the introduction to his preliminary advice spoke volumes about lay participation. He wrote: '*Pour savoir une chose, il faut l'avoir apprise*'. Levy dismissed any notion of lay participation in the administration of justice, 'especially in juries'. He declared that:

> There is no fundamental principle that justifies it [juries]. Granted, they would a) not simplify but complicate the proceedings; b) vulgarise the law that actually strives for the enduring nature of principles; c) make decisions not based on responsibility; d) threaten both legal certainty and unity of law; e) disrupt the rule of law …[3]

It won the day: lay participation in criminal cases was rejected completely. That was in 1908; if less completely, it prevails. The Dutch House of Representatives has recently (2014) decided not to proceed with any proposal for introducing lay adjudication.

III. MODE OF TRIAL

A. The Netherlands

The Dutch criminal justice system makes additional use of honorary judges (*Rechter-plaatsvervanger*) who participate in regular cases in all legal fields. These honorary judges all possess a university degree in law, and they must have been in practice as a lawyer, or a law academic, for at least six years before they can be appointed as honorary judges. Other non-academics and those who are not experts are not involved in the criminal justice system. The Dutch system is thus a conspicuous

---

[2] (2014) 20(1) *Fundamina* 427.
[3] JA Levy, 'Verdient het aanbeveling, het leekenelement aan de rechtspraak … te doen deelnemen?' (1908) I(2) *HNJV* 518–19.

exception, relying on professionalism, unlike other European modes of criminal trial, where amateurism plays a significant part. Participants who have no background in law act as judges, in contrast to the Dutch system. In terms of rationality and logic, the Dutch are right in rejecting the contemporary trend to inject democracy into the trial process. They assume that the administration of justice is not intrinsically a democratic institution, but that it is to be composed of career judges, supplemented on occasion by legally trained persons in academia or private practice; they are dubbed honorary judges.

In research in 2009 Ms Marijke Malsch, a member of the Netherlands Institute for the Study of Crime and Law Enforcement (NSCR),[4] concluded that 'Dutch courts fit very well in the Dutch professionalised legal system'. It was the movement for democratisation of the institution that prompted advocacy for change. While those interviewed for the research were generally content with the system (which the author of the research proclaimed was less than desirable), one honorary judge was quoted[5] as saying that he did not 'understand the current desire to involve lay people in the trial of cases', although he recognised that, politically, the citizen wished to have influence in court decisions. He added that 'the solution would be better sought in improving the legal system. Increasing the quality, giving a rationale for decisions, the apparent fairness of the trial and the integrity of the judges would seem to be a better solution'.

The Dutch assertion precluded any non-legal participation only on the ground of necessity; it did not concede the popular clamour for lay participation on the grounds that favoured their involvement in the criminal trials of fellow citizens. Indeed, one muses that the clamour for lay participation, alongside professional judges, reflects a political will that generally asserts greater and more direct accountability for the verdicts of the criminal courts. It is a sense that mistrusts the exclusivity of the judiciary or any professional expertise that resists lay participation.

It is a fact that the lay element in the Dutch legal system has almost totally disappeared. Participants who have no background in law do, however, act to try agricultural tenancy cases and criminal cases involving the armed forces, or as part of a court that hears cases concerning the execution of sentences in the *Penitentiaire Kamer, Hof Arnhem* (Execution of.Sentences Court). There is also a Companies and Business

---

[4] M Malsch, *Democracy in the Courts (Lay Participation in European Criminal Justice Systems)* (Routledge, 2009) first issued in paperback 2016, 104–16.
[5] ibid, 84.

Court and the Plant Breeders Division. Lay participants may also be involved in procedures such as arbitration and mediation. All these participants, however, lacking legal training, are still experts in their own field of expertise. The honorary judges used in criminal cases do participate in all legal fields. But, in all, there are minimal departures from the insistence on professionals demonstrating a professional skill in the assessment of the credibility and reliability of witnesses in the forum of a criminal trial. The proponents of the Dutch mode of criminal trial consider that to assert the training and qualification of the legal process is a strict requirement of society's attitude to a public institution of constitutional significance. It mirrors social attitudes to the element of a judicature. In this, it adopts the inflexibility of judging in the criminal justice arena.

B. Germany

Lay judges (*Schöffen*) have been the route in Germany and her states throughout their early history and the Middle Ages. The Reich constitution of 1849 provided for both public and oral criminal proceedings, and for jury trial for more serious crimes and political offences. The demand for jury trials was met by the overwhelming majority of German states, which followed (variably according to the individual state) the events of 1848. In 1850 the Kingdom of Hanover provided for the modern alternative to the jury: a criminal court composed of professional and lay judges decided cases in collaboration. After considerable debate the *Schöffengericht* was officially established in 1877 in its jurisdiction over petty crimes. A number of jurisdictional changes took place over the years until 1924 when the jury was transformed into a mixed tribunal composed of three professional judges and six lay judges, the *soi-disant Schwurgericht*. The present organisation dates from 1970. Except for petty crimes (which are tried before a single professional judge) and serious political offences, all crimes are tried by tribunals on which lay judges decide cases together with professional judges. There is also a wide variety of German tribunals with differing compositions.

The lay judges in the German courts have the right to question the accused, other witnesses and experts. They are equally involved in the deliberation and decision-making. In panels with two *Schöffen* and one professional judge, a two-thirds majority is required to reach a decision. Professional judges being outvoted by the two *Schöffen* is rare. Significantly, research shows that in about half of cases the professional judges appear to succeed in changing the lay opinions whenever there is disagreement. Recent research by Marijke Malsch suggests that professional judges' views prevail even where the *Schöffen* have had considerable experience in the adjudication of cases.

The research that emerges from the literature of the most sophisticated modes of mixed tribunals in Germany is that the lay participation element in trials is not without its critics, mainly because of the lack of direct involvement by lay participation. Much of the debate about the validity of the system stems from the general prevalence of the professional judges. It is strongly argued that if the lay participants were better instructed, or were given greater access to the case files, a better balance between the professional judges and the *Schöffen* would be established. The research concludes[6] that

> the literature makes it clear that there is no suggestion of abolishing lay participation. The involvement of lay people in the trial of criminal cases is considerable in Germany. There are, however, a lot more criticisms voiced on the actual contributions of the lay people to the hearing of the case.

This conclusion was reflected in the views of professional and lay persons. 'Professional judges seem considerably more critical of the adjudicatory system than are the *Schöffen* themselves'.[7]

While the public seemed to conclude that professional judges played a dominant part in the mixed tribunal, their satisfaction with the involvement of ordinary citizens in the trial of criminal cases 'was reasonably high'. The principle of participation by lay persons is now well-grounded in the country. The public seems to find the system socially acceptable. This acceptability of criminal court decisions is to be found among defendants and the public, and represents a more positive view of lay participation. By contrast, 'most professionals remain unconvinced that lay participation enhances the quality of the decision'. There are elements of the Dutch approach of an entirely professional court.

C. Belgium

Even before the European Court of Human Rights struck down the Belgian court's decision in *Taxquet* in November 2011 the Belgian Government had begun the reform of the system of jury trial, a variant

[6] ibid, 138.
[7] ibid, 150.

of the Anglo-American version of the jury. Opposing views about the jury were bandied about, opinions wavering about the advantages and disadvantages of the jury. Numerical counting – an impermissible gauge on criminal justice – was overwhelmingly countered by the strikingly different mode of trial from the systems in other European countries of making use of lay judges to balance the professionalism of courts, the participation of lay persons in criminal justice. The neighbouring systems – apart from the Dutch – had strongly insisted on a much more introverted institution that hardly attracted any media attention, unlike jury trials (certainly before the end in England of capital punishment in 1965) which were extroverted by the important role the print media played in disseminating information about what happened in the court-room. The thespian aspects of Belgian trials which were active prompted the lessening of dramatics inherent in trials and emotional drama, noticeably absent after 1965 in England. Even then, the dramatic quali-ties of defence lawyers did not disappear. In my few years of experience of jury trials in England, the impression borne upon me by my legal colleagues was that of actors manqués. When confronted with their ambitions to achieve acquittals for their clients, many defence counsel (not so jokingly) thought that their ultimate duty was to throw up the biggest smokescreen in front of the jury; often that device was successful as a distortion of the true circumstances of the criminal event.[8]

The Belgian solution was to obliterate such devices and to persuade jurors that they contributed to verdicts that assisted defendants. These reforms were aptly directed to procedure during the evidence and the final submissions by defence counsel. Less attention was paid to the quality of any jury deliberation and the absence of a reasoned verdict. The establishment in Belgium of lay participation in criminal trials had the benefit of encouraging future comparative research into mixed tribunals.

D. Denmark

Research into trials with lay participation seemed, contrariwise, to find that faith in the jury system was exceptionally high. The Danish judicial

---

[8] Jeremy Bentham – no friend of the legal profession – once wrote that it is the intent of every advocate that every 'right and wrong should be confused as contradictory or unsettled and in his hands as pliant as possible'.

culture seems to have readily endorsed the dual function of professionals and amateurs; the culture accepts the mixed tribunal in which the
judiciary is not accorded so high a reputation. The participation of lay
persons in various social institutions is self-evident; criminal justice fits
into that picture of Danish society. There appears to be a negative assertion of the fear of judicial dominance, although no system is free of some
criticism. Most of the complaints focused on the quality of deliberation
by lay persons. The overriding picture, without any adverse comment
to the quality of reasoned verdicts, is of social satisfaction; there is no
movement to alter the system.

E. France

The French jury is the paradigm 'mixed' jury of the European systems.
Three professional judges sit with nine lay jurors, all of whom are
randomly selected from lists of eligible voters to sit for singular cases.
Judges and jurors deliberate together about questions of guilt and
punishment, and must agree by a margin of at least 8–4 to convict the
defendant. Failure to reach the required majority leads to an acquittal or
to lesser punishment. Notably, the deliberation is secret, and the ultimate
vote is taken in private. Since unanimity is not required, therefore, jurors
and judges do not know how their co-panellists have voted.

Acting on the decision of the Strasbourg court that defendants should
always be in a position of understanding the verdicts of their trial,
France and other countries overwhelmed their jury system by imposing
a 'reason-giving' requirement on criminal trial verdicts. The reform was
purportedly motivated by the desire, described as a moral precept, in
the process of decision-making and deliberation, to give reasons for the
verdict. The legislators wanted to enhance the contemporary rule. While
its primary purpose was to expand the human rights of the defendant,
by repairing the present defect of the system, the *travaux preparatoires*
demonstrated that the legislation had two purposes. Apart from filling
the gap of dubious 'reason-giving' in the system, until the 2011 reform
not at all, French courts likewise gave written reasons for their verdicts;
the wide variation in reason-giving between courts in this procedure
meant that defendants charged with the more serious criminal offences
(and facing the prospect of longer prison sentences) were not entitled
to reasons, unlike others facing charges on lesser offences. A second
reform has to include appeals. For most of their history, French jury
verdicts could only be appealed to the *Cour de cassation*, France's court

of last resort for criminal and civil matters. The *Cour de cassation* operates under a rigorous, deferential standard, strictly limiting any review to compliance and procedural law based on the proceedings in the court below. In 2000, to comply with the principle in the ECHR of the right to appeal, France introduced a new intermediate appeals procedure. Both prosecution and defence can now appeal as a matter of right.

Against the background of these two reforms for the rights of defendants, there emerged in France a more complicated story. On the one hand, there appeared to be a system of reason-giving in jury trials as a purely humanitarian position, in accordance with the *Taxquet* finding. On the other hand, a practice in the criminal administration of seeking stricter mechanisms of judicial accountability has been exhibited. The requirement that mixed juries explain their verdicts can be seen not only as a pro-defendant commitment but also as a means of administrative convenience and court-control. Whether or not these prevail, the real or imagined qualities of the jury system and the effect of reason-giving on the ineligibility of verdicts with concepts of judicial power and rule over the lay persons remain unresolved. An article in 2016 by Mathilde Cohen, 'The French Case for Requiring Juries to Give Reasons: Safeguarding Defendants or Guarding the Judges?'[9] supports the limited role of reason-giving.

The problems of determining the decision-making between the professional judiciary and the lay participants are once more at play; they constitute the legitimacy of the mixed tribunal for the trial of serious criminal offences.

F. Scotland

As in England and Wales, there seems to be a general acceptance that for serious criminal offences there is no acceptable alternative of juryless trial. Although the legal system in Scotland adopts in principle the European Roman-Dutch system, and negates any lay participation in its criminal courts, it generally follows the English model of jury trial with slight modifications. There are formally two versions of

---

[9] M Cohen, 'The French Case for Requiring Juries to Give Reasons: Safeguarding Defendants or Guarding the Judges?' in JE Ross and SC Thaman (eds), *Comparative Criminal Procedure* (Edward Elgar Publishing, 2016) 422.

an acquittal – either the defendant is not guilty, or, exceptionally, the prosecution's case is not proven. Notably, the mode of trial does not accept any alternative to a verdict rendered by a simple majority, for which there must be eight out of the 15 jurors. In May 2017 the High Court in Glasgow concluded a criminal trial lasting 320 days. Although lengthy trials are rare, the case is likely to renew criticism of the delay and the general cost of modernising justice, and suggestions of some shorter form of criminal trial, which must of course be fair.

The absence from the jury verdict of any reasoned judgment is, however, a constant theme of some critics. While the European Court of Human Rights has so far refused to admit a case challenging the unreasoned verdict of a Scottish trial, in *Judge v The United Kingdom*[10] the ECHR noted that the appellate system in Scotland, which oversees the place of the jury, was neither logistically inconsistent nor irrational as a safeguard against aberrations.

The sole concern in Scotland seems to be the rule of corroboration of evidence. Governmental desire to reverse the verdict, which does not pertain in England, failed to attain parliamentary success, whence the Government set up a commission to review the Scottish system for trying serious crimes. One of the oddities of prosecutorial procedure in Scotland is worthy of mention. Unlike in England, where the Director of Public Prosecutions has a discretion whether to launch proceedings for an indictable offence (in such capacity he expresses the decisions of an independent agent, and not a servant of government), in Scotland there is no discretion whether to charge the offender; the prosecution is part of the service of the Lord Advocate. The prosecution, therefore, denotes that the defendant has a duty to undergo jury trial. Contrariwise, advocates in England claim, probably wrongly, that the accused has a *right* to jury trial. If that is the correct verdict, there must be left to the accused the decision whether he wishes to undergo trial by jury. Choice of mode of trial would seem to exist.

Every modern system of criminal justice depends on lay participation – whether in the whole trial in the Anglo-American systems, or lay participation in the trial process to buttress hierarchically judicial functions. In the jury system in England, there is an implacable acknowledgment of a monosyllabic verdict: no reasons for the verdict are required, or, indeed, may even be given, formally or informally. In the mixed tribunals there is a requirement of a reasonable form of reasons, but their adequacy

---

[10] 2011 SCCR 241, (2011) 52 EHRR SE17, ECtHR.

remains to be authoritatively spelt out by the European Court of Human Rights. In a literate society in which scientific and technological issues abound and cost increasingly matters for expert testimony, criminal offences are more susceptible to reasoned verdicts demanding the expertise of professionalism.

IV. CONCLUSION

Criminal liability is determinable exclusively by a court of law; no other body can dispense criminal justice establishing a fair trial before an independent and impartial judiciary. As an institution established as part of the administration of justice in the tripartite arm of modern government, the criminal court constitutes no democratic principle, as a necessity, although most modern democracies (but not all, at all times) inject into their systems of criminal justice an element of lay participation, in various forms. It is a misapplication, treated as if criminal justice needed a dosage of democracy, whereas the choice of those tribunals is between professionalism and the insertion of amateurism of the lay participation in the quality of justice. It is a confusion of the legal principle of due process.

The aim of the criminal court is to ensure a high quality of legal service by a tribunal composed of persons qualified and skilled in the forensic process, undiluted by any lay intervention. The trial procedure encompasses a capacity to assess the credibility and reliability of witnesses and conclude in a professionally reasoned verdict. Without reasons for the determination of guilt or innocence the process is socially unacceptable as lacking full transparency and accountability if it involves the amateurism of lay participation – 'real' live persons. Any lay participation in the mode of criminal trial, either wholly by jurors (as in the Anglo-Saxon systems) or as a proportion of persons alongside the judiciary, involves the problems of the relationship of the actors.

Would, moreover, any injection of lay participation in the process of determining guilt or innocence qualify as a fair trial under Article 6 of the European Convention on Human Rights? That poses the persistent argument of the appropriate mode of criminal trial. Among models of courts in criminal justice, the Dutch system uniquely for two centuries has observed the concept of professionalism among its panellists as full-time (or, exceptionally, honorary) judges. Adherence to its judicial set-up has been resoundingly affirmed in recent times.

Proponents of democratic principles as a part of the court process regard as essential in modern trials of serious criminal offences three identifiable aspects (see Marijke Malsch in her valuable study and review of the European systems, *Democracy in the Courts*,[11] who asserts that lay participation is entirely desirable in modern societies). The results of her identification of the three elements of lay participation are, she admits, 'not very encouraging';[12] all systems pose practical problems of merging judicial and non-legal powers in the trial process.

Participation by lay persons provides a variable amount of lay involvement in the criminal court. The practical problems associated with determining which class of citizens should take part in any adjudication abound in the various systems. What precise part should the judges play in the total decision with the lay persons, such as evaluating evidence? Also, lay participation in the deliberative process has aroused many problems about the distribution of voting power. Above all, the articulation of the reasoned verdict looms large in post-trial results. The giving of reasons raises insoluble problems. Should the drafting be initiated by the professional judge(s)? Are the lay participants properly involved in the reasoning process? If opinion is divided, how is the verdict resolved? It is not surprising that the requirement of reasonable reasons for a verdict involving lay participants has caused criticism of the process.

Professor Corjo Jansen, a legal historian at Nijmegen University, alludes in his 2014 essay 'The Participation of Laymen in the Dutch Judiciary (1811–2011)'[13] that the Dutch system is unique in Europe. Nothing in the Dutch Constitution (section 116(3)) actually prevents any lay administration of justice, 'but the trend towards lay participation seems to have been reversed, at least politically'. There is hence no dissatisfaction with the system. It appears to be effective. Professionalism in the criminal process maintains its value in at least one civilised system of criminal justice.

This author does not disguise his approval for professionalism in the principle of due process. Already specific offences – particularly in the realm of fraud – are singled out for juryless trials. Other criminalities require specialist views through experts; as such may there not be some reform of the system of trial to accommodate the growing specialists in litigation?

---

[11] Malsch, *Democracy in the Courts (Lay Participation in European Criminal Justice Systems)* n 4 above.
[12] ibid, 193.
[13] See n 2 above.

5

The Value of the Mixed (Lay Participation) Tribunal

IT WOULD BE foolish to ignore, let alone discount effectively, the contribution which the unqualified lay person can bring to the prime aim of a criminal court to assess the credibility and reliability of the testimony of a witness, in documents or orally. This is particularly so where the criminal offence in question involves issues of domesticity under the purview of communal living; it would be otherwise in the case of corporate fraud where the issues would be unlikely to occur in the daily experience of the lay person. Even where the fact-finding process of the trial encompasses the experience of ordinary community living, there is always the factor of professional superiority, the awesomeness of the judicial chamber over the unqualified lay person. But overall, one would concede that there is a positive virtue in bringing to bear on such questions the views of the ordinary citizen. One need not invoke the principle of democracy to argue in favour of a mixture of talents, even if the lay perception finds the scene of the courtroom somewhat unnerving as an unusual experience. It is a basic element of civil society that the populace should get a taste of the forensic forum, with all its trappings of a major public institution.

In his, admittedly limited, survey of information on the jury systems used in 28 democratic countries, Associate Professor Ethan J Leib concludes that there is clear evidence 'that criminal justice systems are not necessary to the design of democratic polities'.[1] He adds:

> No one should think a criminal jury is a necessary qualification for a democracy in the contemporary global community. Indeed, about half of the big democracies reject jury systems altogether. Lay adjudication in some form certainly appears dominant among the world's democracies [no doubt having a salutary effect], but the form that lay adjudication takes varies a great deal.

---

[1] EJ Leib, 'A Comparison of Criminal Jury Decision Rules in Democratic Countries' (2007–2008) 5 *Ohio State Journal of Criminal Law* 629.

The model that is frequently mooted – 'the jury of one's peers' – is hardly a marker of the democratic, whatever else the rhetorical phrase may impart.

It is the second element in the trial of a criminal offender that arouses misgivings about the validity of the trial process. That is the declaration of a verdict, based exclusively on the material adduced in the courtroom, and the reasoning of whatever is the outcome of the voting by the judicial members or the lay participants. Every consideration of this points to the disadvantage of the unqualified. Apart from the proper presentation of the reasoned decision (particularly if the voting is split), the plain fact is that only the judges have the necessary expertise to frame the document that explains why and how evidence has been evaluated and assessed, and are almost certain to dominate. Not just the framing of the reasons but the manner in which the reasons are considered will inevitably carry the hallmark of judicial dominance. It may not always be so, but the composition of the mixed tribunal inevitably sets the professional skills and judgment of the lawyer alongside any appropriate attributes that the lay participants may bring.

Overall, however, the account must come down in favour of professionalism. The whole process of criminal proceedings, as a valuable institution of criminal justice, is couched in legal terms, including the nature and scope of the criminal offence. It is not a process for the control of crime in society. It is exclusively concerned with ensuring a fair trial. The experience in criminal justice of a formalised trial is alien to the lay participant. To implement the habits of legal training, constant experience in the courtroom and a sense of understanding of the criminal process, in all its ramifications of investigation, prosecution and presentation within a human rights concept, gives the judge an understanding and appreciation that will not readily be adopted by the lay participant. As the Dutch system evokes, the trial of a serious criminal offence is quintessentially an aspect of public administration, for which the State is answerable.

My conclusion is that, on balance, professionalism must be the order of the day. That is not to say that trial by judges suffices to account for the trial of criminals, and that transparency is sufficient. Both attributes need close attention and full application in a 'fair trial'. A totally judge-composed tribunal must always contain a single judge,[2] and on appeal

---

[2] I think that there is room for arguing for no more than a single judge for the trial process. It worked effectively in Northern Ireland in the Diplock Courts and other exceptional juryless trials.

no fewer than three judges, of whom one may be (as in The Netherlands) an honorary judge. Every verdict (of guilt or innocence) must be fully reasoned and be subject to appeal in the same way as the civil court jurisdiction. An acquittal must also be appealable by the prosecution. There is no place in a civilised system for the nullification of a perverse acquittal.

If every indictable offence invites a trial before three judges, that situation may not always pertain. Whatever the logic and legitimacy advanced for abolition of the system of jury trial, it is nevertheless compelling that there remains today a public devotion – I use that word deliberately, as indicating a profound belief – to the Anglo-Saxon trial by one's peers. Politics – the art of the possible, RAB Butler declared – demands that the citizen should be allowed the choice of putting his defence to a serious criminal charge before 12 citizens, democratically selected from the electoral roll, with suitable quali-fications. The proposal that a defendant should be allowed to elect jury trial is not new. Many countries operate a waiver system that provides for what is called a Bench trial. As long ago as 1843, Jeremy Bentham proclaimed the absurdity of trial by jury; he added that, if anyone wanted that system he should be allowed to insist upon it. Properly regulated, a defendant should be allowed to keep trial by his own peers, recognising that he thereby forgoes the valuable right to know why he has been found guilty, or indeed innocent. The presence of the unreasoned verdict of a silent juror is not tenable in a modern society which rightly places a good deal in its education system on any decision-maker explaining fully how he arrives at the verdict of crimi-nality. But that inarticulateness in jury trial is concomitant with the system. Choose the system and you inevitably forgo the normality of reasons for the decision. We demand nothing less in our civil system of law. The criminal jurisdiction must now follow suit.

6

The Tale of Taxquet

WHEN THE DRAFTSMEN of the European Convention on Human Rights conceived of the human right to a fair trial under Article 6, they wisely did no more than say that criminal justice should be based on the model of existing tribunals – variations reflecting cultural and historical peculiarities, the defining feature of which is that, mostly, professional judges are unable *alone* to determine the jurors' deliberation on their verdict. For 60 years, the Strasbourg Court declined to identify the various models, only to assert that, whatever kind of court the members of the Council of Europe chose to effect enforcement of serious crime, it had always to be conducted fairly. *Taxquet v Belgium* on 16 November 2010 positively declined to question the operation of the jury system as such. The court would examine whether sufficient procedural guarantees were in place in the particular case before it.

When, in November 2010, the Grand Chamber of the European Court of Human Rights declined to assess and evaluate the various models extant in western Europe, it focused entirely on the ingredients of a fair trial by the independence and impartiality of municipal systems in implementing the European Convention on Human Rights. For any view about the modes of criminal trial, it quoted the arguments of the Irish Government (acting as a third party intervenor in the instant case) enunciating the Anglo-Saxon adherence to the decision of 12 lay jurors. It said:

> In the Irish Government's submission, the system of jury trial in Ireland was the unanimous choice of accused persons and of human rights advocates of the country's criminal law system. There had never been a complaint that the system lacked transparency or impinged on or inhibited the rights of the accused. The system inspired confidence among the Irish people who were very attached to it for historical and other reasons ... The Irish Government wondered how a system of trial that had been in operation for centuries

[inherited from England in 1922, on independence] and long pre-dated the Convention could now be considered to breach article 6(1).[1]

Contemporaneously, on the day of the Grand Chamber's judgment, the opinion of Lord Judge, the distinguished Lord Chief Justice of England and Wales, similarly prompted the English support of the Irish view. He said that the judges of the Grand Chamber understood clearly that the jury system, as it operates in the English jurisdiction, could not be brushed aside. In a speech on jury trials (in his Judicial Studies Board lecture to a Belfast audience) he said that a properly structured summing-up, followed by a verdict of the jury, which is confined to the verdict, provides the public and the accused with sufficient understanding of the undisclosed reasons of the jury's verdict. The opposite conclusion is that the unknown reception by the jury of the direction in law and the summing-up on the relevant facts for decision-making is often ineffective, if not actually ineffectual. Furthermore, unless and until we are possessed of information about the dialectic effect of the chemistry of judge and jury we are bereft of translating views about the reliability of jury trial into the reality of what lies behind the monosyllabic utterance of the unreasoned verdict. Meanwhile, there is an insistence on fairness in the adjudication of the courts of the legal system. Such utterances have been aired by members of the judiciary, in an extra-curricular fashion.

The latest Devlinesque pronouncement to support the jury system came from Lady Justice Hallett in a lecture on 23 May 2017 at Pembroke College, Cambridge. She asserted that jury trials were 'another form of democracy – members of the public sitting on a jury as the democratic branch of the judiciary'. She went on to assert that a juror 'is part of the delivery of justice, and that is itself an aspect of participatory democracy'. She was wrong, on both counts.

The jury, historically, was never part of the judiciary. Until the Criminal Justice Act 1972 it was not even democratic. Only property owners qualified for jury service; only widows and spinsters could sit as jurors, otherwise juries consisted of 'men only'.[2] Even then they were seen as being 'dispensed on high by what might be described pejoratively as an unaccountable elite'. They were, before 1972, an 'unelected' group of the ruling power. The instrument of criminal justice has never been dubbed 'democratic', although legislators are entitled to insert an

---

[1] *Taxquet v Belgium* (GC) (2012) 54 EHRR 26, para 78.
[2] Under the Irish Constitution, only men qualified.

element of democratic power into a judicial model. But democracy has never been a part of the judicature as an arm of civilised government. Jury trial, moreover, cannot be described as the lay person's participation in criminal trials. Juries predominate as the exclusive decision-maker; it is not participation – it is wholesale occupancy of the unaccountable verdict, and judicially unaided, when promoted in the summing-up.

Jury trial may have its self-justification, like the Star Chamber. But it hardly qualifies as a 'fair trial before an independent and impartial tribunal'. Independence it may claim. But impartiality? I doubt that any body of 12 people drawn randomly and untested can claim neutrality about the commission of a criminal offence. Indeed, its virtue may lie in its sense of the public interest to control crime.

The process of criminal justice is the direct product of an administrative penal system. As such it is an instrument that belongs to the state in its function as protector of individual harm by other citizens. Its aim is to perform its prime role of serving the safety of its citizenry as the victims of crime. In a sense, the state establishes a system of criminal court as part of the official remedy available to the victim.

Meanwhile, the aims for a fair trial depend on the procedural guarantees that imply a sense of reasons for the verdict. But procedural guarantees, such as the right of an accused to face his accusers in the courtroom, are essential. Procedures, however, call for understanding from both the skilled decision-maker, as much as if not more than the unskilled observer of credibility and reliability of evidence adduced in the forum of the criminal trial, with all its official trappings, like the dock (enclosed or open, with legal assistance). In short, the art of judiciality must be a primary function of the tribunal. And judiciality is attained only by training and experience; it is a conspicuously individual approach, but not (at least not easily) shared. Moreover, a guilty verdict which does not intrinsically contain the reasoning that convinces the reader cannot, therefore, be appealed against, unlike a body with full jurisdiction that reveals the whys and wherefores of guilt. Appellate functions provide an added ground for insisting on a reasoned verdict, if only its susceptibility to judicial review. Above all, *Taxquet* acknowledges, pointedly, that a reasoned court decision formed part of the guarantee for a fair trial. It would be illogical for the law to be less so for proceedings resulting in the severity of penal sanctions for crime.

For the moment (in 2018) it seems not to be the function of the European Court of Human Rights to standardise the various models of criminal justice within the Council of Europe. Its function is, however, to elucidate the international law of human rights reflected in the

Convention, without any regard to the functions performed by municipal courts. It is the arbiter of human rights; it has, therefore, sensibly adopted the doctrine of margins of appreciation. The result of a trial process is firmly accorded to the municipal court, taking into account the human rights jurisprudence of Strasbourg. As the judgment in *Taxquet* puts it:

> ... the institution of the lay jury cannot be called into question ... The Contracting States enjoy considerable freedom in the choice of the means calculated to ensure that their judicial systems are in compliance with the requirements of Article 6. The Court's task is to consider whether the method adopted to that end has led in a given case to results which are compatible with the Convention, while also taking into account the specific circumstances, the nature and complexity of the case. In short, it must ascertain whether the proceedings as a whole were fair.[3]

As always, when addressing a decision from the court at Strasbourg, the UK court's attention must be fact-specific for the case to be relevant. Hence, after the delivery of the *Taxquet* judgment, the UK courts explained its limited function. In *R v Lawless*,[4] the Court of Appeal explained the function of the summing-up to the jury. Since there was no clarity about the nature of the case against the accused, or the jury's conclusion to the weight of that evidence (since the jury is not required to give its reasons, or what each juror thought of each piece of evidence), the verdict was upheld. Helpfully, the English Court of Appeal underlined that there was not in English law a duty to give reasons, and it declared that there was no reason to suppose that that state of affairs was likely to change in the immediate future, at least not as a result of the decision in *Taxquet*. Later, in March 2011, the Court of Appeal, in *R v Chomir Ali*,[5] held that a format of a route to verdict, suggested as a way of supplying a safeguard in the absence of a reasoned verdict, should be rejected. It added that in the instant case there was no doubt that a route-to-verdict document would in fact have complicated the jury's task, rather than simplified it. That did not rule out that such a document may often be of enormous help to juries in criminal trials.

But *Taxquet* did appear to establish one vital procedural principle, in enunciating that criminal defendants ought always to 'understand' jury verdicts. The European Court of Human Rights declared criminal courts

---

[3] At para 84.
[4] *R v Lawless* [2011] EWCA Crim 59, (2011) 175 JP 93.
[5] *R v Chomir Ali* [2011] EWCA Crim 1011.

should ensure that their 'reason-giving' appeared to represent, by implication in the Convention, an individual human right which could be linked to the municipal criminal law, exceptionally. Decision-makers ought to be particularly careful in their decision-making and the explanations for those decisions, because the potential deprivation of the defendant's liberty is being legitimised by the verdict of guilt. The defendant's interest in personal autonomy is at stake, through a process compelling defendants to extrapolate the reasons for their conviction and sentence (for which there is in England compliance, since it is the exclusive power of the trial judge). The absence of reasons from the trial process calls for a need to perfect the fairness of a trial. As a matter of crucial completeness, the European Court of Human Rights has held that, as a matter of fundamental human rights, defendants must be able to understand what has led to their conviction. There have been some helpful suggestions whereby the jury might be required to give an explanation of its reasons. In Sir Brian Leveson's *Review of Efficiency in Criminal Proceedings* (January 2015), he recommends[6] that jurors should be given a series of written factual statements; and that the 'route to verdict' should be clear enough that the defendant and the public 'may understand the basis for the verdict that has been reached', a repeat of the words of the European Court of Human Rights in the *Taxquet* case.

It is no little wonder that the European Union (Withdrawal) Bill in July 2017 did not include, for transfer from European law into UK law, the Charter for Fundamental Rights, Article 47 of which, additional to Article 6 of the European Convention on Human Rights, provides a stronger protection of the right to a fair trial. Article 47 is not restricted to cases concerning a person's determination of his civil rights and obligations or of any criminal charge against him. The protection under Article 47 is therefore wider in scope than that under Article 6 of European Convention on Human Rights and includes administrative proceedings, such as those on tax or immigration. Significantly, the protection impacts on the right to a fair trial in applying the mode of trial. In short, the law of the Court of Justice of the European Union states that the national member's procedures must ensure that the person concerned must be informed of the essence of the ground which constitutes the basis of the decision. Reasons, at least reasonably given, constitute the basis of the tribunal's decision. The verdict is accorded something more than being pronounced. It needs to be substantiated expressionally. Underlining is not an ideal exercise.

---

[6] At paras 385–88.

The greatest single defect in the process of jury trial, as identified in the fairness of the trial, is the lack of reasons for the jury's verdict. That was noted by Lord Brown of Eaton-under-Heywood in a lecture in Oxford in October 2010, commenting on the *Taxquet* case in the European Court of Human Rights. From the judgment of the First Chamber of the court, Lord Brown cited a passage. The seven European judges stated:

> In its case-law the Court has frequently held that the reasoning provided in court decisions is closely linked to the concern to ensure a fair trial ... Such a reasoning is essential to the very quality of justice and provides a safeguard against arbitrariness.

The Court's judgment concluded that Mr Taxquet had been unable to understand the court's decision. This is particularly significant because the jury did not reach its verdict on the basis of the evidence.

A year later the Grand Chamber upheld the appeal on the ground that to constitute a fair trial, the accused must clearly understand – and therefore accept – the verdict of the trial court.

Eight years have elapsed since the decision in the *Taxquet* case. Despite the tradition of jury trials in common law systems, the right to a fair trial under Article 6 of European Convention on Human Rights does not guarantee a right to trial by jury. In *R v Twomey*,[7] the Court of Appeal (contemporaneously to the *Taxquet* case) stated that for the purposes of the fairness of the trial under Article 6 of the Convention, 'it is irrelevant whether the tribunal is judge and jury, or judge alone'.

The debate is about the mode of trial in criminal justice. It is not a comparison of processes of investigation of crime and its prosecution. Thus the rejection of the method of trial in most of western Europe is focused on the effectiveness and legitimacy of the police and the prosecution service, in which there is discussion between the prosecutor and the defence. The inquisitorial approach to the process of criminal justice faces different challenges from those of the adversarial system in the face of the adjudicating court.

That is the scope of *Taxquet* and the limit of Article 6 of the European Convention on Human Rights. However much longer one must wait for it, the urge for municipal change is ripe. The long history of jury trial may be obsolescent, but its further continuance will demand its reform.

---

[7] *R v Twomey* [2009] EWCA Crim 1035, [2010] 1 WLR 630, at para 18.

7

Juryless Trials: Diplock Courts and Others

WHEN THE BRITISH Army was ordered by the UK Government in December 1969 to confront the growing civil disturbances in Northern Ireland, thereby acting throughout the Troubles as 'an aid to the civil power' of the Royal Ulster Constabulary, the principles of criminal justice were inevitably at risk. Trial by jury for serious crimes was a major target for change, given its inability to convict or acquit equitably and without hint of prejudice those accused of terrorist activities in a deeply divided society. Internment of August 1971 in the Province further confirmed the abandonment of the rights of the defence involving lay participation in the aim of a fair trial. But was it more than a severely practical response to the influx of unacceptable verdicts of juries in a divided country? Or was the reform an experiment into alternative modes of a fair trial? If a return to jury trial would be restored after the emergency, was it not a test?

It was unsurprising that the Departmental Committee under Lord Diplock in 1972 reported about the ineffectiveness of jury trial over emergency cases, and strongly urged the replacement of jury trial by a mode of trial that instituted trial by judge alone, with the specific requirement of a reasoned verdict, reviewable on appeal. Given the overwhelming support for jury trial, the reform was nevertheless socially acceptable only for as long as the disturbances persisted. It was generally accepted that jury trial would be reinstated when the emergency was ended. The year 2007 saw the return of jury trial. If the 30 years of juryless trial for designated crime was decidedly not an experiment in modes of trial being conducted professionally, the experience of the system of Diplock Courts cannot be ignored. The extensive use of juryless trials, even in the limited application of criminal justice, may have demonstrated the effectiveness of a professional mode of criminal trial. The special court of judge alone was anticipated as reflecting times of national emergency cases. It was an experiment in juryless trials, however long the Diplock Courts lasted.

The concept of juryless trials is certainly not unknown to English law, but its application has been severely restricted to cases where trial by jury is demonstrably at risk from the intimidation of jurors. The jurisprudence of a limited use of any trial by judge alone is outspoken on the notion of the jury system. It is certainly not an example of the alternative of professionalism over amateurism. The voice as a mark of popularism remains largely undimmed. Attempts at broadening the limited scope of trial by judge alone were the subject of government and parliamentary activity in the last decade of the twentieth century; the legislative battle was lost in 2007 with the lapse of the Fraud (Trials) Bill. That failure was an example of trying to persuade the country to cover other issues where trial by jury was thought to be an impossible burden in complicated cases facing the courts, such as fraud on a corporate scale. Departure in principle from the normal trial by jury was evidenced by the time limit prescribed.

An unreasoned verdict by the jurors of the Middle Ages, from an illiterate society, may well have sufficed in such an unenlightened society. But can it now be socially acceptable? It is entirely feasible that one can infer the reasons for a jury's unreasoned verdict from the evidential material digested by the jurors. So long, therefore, as the quality and complexity of the material is readily encompassed, trial by jury is tenable. Any kind of inquiry that relies on the facts that need clarification and analysis involves a process of reasoning, a ratiocination of the monosyllabic verdict. Anything less than that ratiocination cannot suffice the recipient of the unreasoned verdict; he needs the wherewithal to fathom or test out the strands of the variegated evidence. The distinction between the jury verdict and an understanding of that verdict (acceptably analysed in a summing-up by the judge) is one thing. But at least the authors of the Northern Ireland (Emergency Provisions) Act 1973 thought otherwise. All the juryless Diplock Courts demanded that the ultimate judgment must be reasoned, whether a verdict of guilt or of innocence from the professional tribunal.

The enduring, even overriding aspect of the indeterminate lifetime over 30 years of the Troubles in Northern Ireland, was that reasons specifically had to be given to accompany the result of a Diplock Court. Even if the judicially reasoned decisions dispensed with the unreasoned verdicts of juries, the tribunals were designedly imposed for a restricted time-scale, and the practical consequences of the procedural requirement of full appellate rights to the defendants in place of their right to trial by jury had a significance beyond their limited lifespan. The history of 30 years of juryless trials tells its own tale.

The temporary nature of the reasoned judgment has had an impact on comparative decisions on the mode of criminal trial. The committee that proposed the establishment of the Diplock Courts expressed no aim other than the pragmatism of professional criminal courts; it certainly expressed no adverse comments on jury trial for such cases as a continuance of civil disorder that assumed the right to social acceptability. The committee merely determined that it was not reasonably possible to get verdicts from a criminally divided populace.

In December 1972 a Commission on legal procedures to deal with terrorist activities, under the chairmanship of Lord Diplock, a distinguished Law Lord, recommended the abandonment of the traditional mode of trial by judge and jury for serious terrorist crimes. It did so for severely pragmatic reasons. The threat of intimidation – even murder – of witnesses, which had been identified, extended also to jurors (though not to the same extent). One provision in the Criminal Justice Bill restricting jury trial was based on similar evidence from Chief Constables that jurors were being intimidated. The Commission said that the threat was a serious one:

> ... particularly to those who live in so-called 'Catholic areas' when a Republican terrorist is on trial, and, more important, is the widespread fear of it ... The result ... is that juries who have tried Republican terrorists, who until recently have been almost the only detected perpetrators of terrorist crimes, have been juries the great majority, if not all, of whom have been Protestants.

Thus, for the duration of the Troubles, the Commission recommended that, for scheduled offences (scheduled by the Attorney-General), trial by judge alone should replace trial by jury. The *soi-disant* Diplock Courts were accordingly brought into existence, providing for safeguards to be put in place to avoid perverse verdicts and the intimidation of jurors.

The Diplock Courts had two distinguishing features. First, the trial judge was required to provide a judgment stating the reasons for a conviction (reasons were normally also given in the case of acquittals). Second, the convicted terrorist had an unqualified right of appeal against both conviction and sentence. Both these requirements, in theory if not in practice, constituted extra safeguards which are absent from the inscrutable verdict of the jury, whose unarticulated decision is inviolate as the sole fact-finder, and, therefore, not readily overturned by the appellate court.

Another dominant feature of the Diplock Court was the retention of the ordinary procedure and practice in criminal trials on indictment.

Its rules of evidence and process were precisely the same – with the removal only of the fundamental component of the court composition. The fact-finding process passed from the jury to the judge who thereby acted as both master of the law (as he was in a jury trial) and the arbiter of the facts. There were other minor differences. But in essence the single judge became both judge and jury. Professor Jackson and his co-author, Sean Doran, in *Judge without Jury: Diplock Trials in the Adversary System*[1] concluded their impressive study in 1995 with the thought that 'trial without jury need not remain transfixed as at present by the jury's spectre' – a clear acceptance that the legislature would reconstruct the adversarial process of trial to suit the functions of a professional tribunal administering criminal justice in the twenty-first century. Advocates before the Diplock Courts have testified to their quality of justice. By implication, barristers are more at home conducting a dialogue with the judge than attempting to persuade the inexperienced jurors, in the role of monologist. The drama of jury trial disappeared.

Allegations of a number of wrongful convictions were made. But a report in 1990 of the Diplock Court system, by the independent reviewer of the emergency legislation, Viscount Colville of Culcross, observed that there was little demand at the time, on the grounds of performance, for an end to the judge-alone trial system. In support, he drew attention to the report by a team of US lawyers in 1987 to the Association of the Bar of the City of New York. This report, from instinctive critics of British policy in Northern Ireland, noted that no one had pointed to a single wrongful conviction of the Diplock system. The same could not have been said a decade later. Allegations of miscarriages of justice were made, and substantiated in at least one case. But, as Jackson and Doran observed: 'It must be said that there has been nothing like the number of claims – many substantiated – in England and Wales in recent years'. Jackson and Doran concluded, moreover, that the aspect of Diplock Court cases which did arouse adverse comment tended to focus on the way judges handled matters within their own province – namely, matters of law, rather than on the assessment and evaluation of the facts enunciated in their judgments. Appellate courts are capable of curing such errors of the trial court. The question instantly arises: would the accused terrorists have fared any better, had they been tried by juries? We cannot tell. But the quality of justice in Northern Ireland was undeniably of a high order.

[1] J Jackson and S Doran, *Judge without Jury: Diplock Trials in the Adversary System* (Oxford, Clarendon Press, 1995).

I. MATERIAL FACTS

To make any valuable assessment of the Diplock system, it was necessary to request information under the Freedom of Information Act 2000. Five main questions were put to the Northern Ireland Office. They were:

(1)   the total number of cases heard by the Diplock Courts over the period during which such courts were functioning;

(2)   how many cases were heard within the Diplock Courts each year from commencement to termination of the Courts' activities;

(3)   of the cases heard in each year, how many of those cases resulted in convictions and how many in acquittals;

(4)   in respect of those matters where there were convictions, please identify how many of those were subsequently heard by the Court of Appeal;

(5)   of the cases which went to the Court of Appeal following conviction, the number of convictions upheld and those quashed.

In its reply of 16 May 2018 the Office stated that it did not hold statistics on convictions for scheduled offences from 1973–1977, but indicated that the National Archives might hold some information. A list of those references covered four periods, as follows:

CJ4/1236, which runs from 10 December 1974–30 June 1976;

CJ4/1238, which runs from 3 September 1975–9 December 1976;

CJ4/1337, which runs from 17 October 1975–22 September 1976;

CJ4/1763, which runs from 26 July 1976–17 January 1977.

The letter helpfully added:

> Following a search of NIO records, a list of prosecutions and convictions for scheduled offences at the Crown Court 'Diplock Courts' from 1978–1983 can be found in the table below.

Year	Prosecutions	Convictions
1978	956	837
1979	922	844
1980	585	550
1981	598	562
1982	793	744
1983	638	577

This data can hardly supply the evidential material of cases over 30 years, but it does suggest at least some conclusions. Over the period of 1978–1983, the Diplock Courts brought in over 4,000 guilty verdicts in nearly 5,000 trials, a conviction rate of approximately 82 per cent, not seriously dissimilar from ordinary jury trial convictions.

The Northern Ireland Office, in its consultation paper of August 2006, proclaiming the arrangements for replacing the Diplock system prior to its abolition the following year, did at least indicate in an annex to the report some pertinent comments from Lord Carlile of Berriew, the Independent Reviewer of Terrorism Legislation. Lord Carlile stated (at paragraph 26)

> that he had received no convincing arguments on the merits in favour of a 3-judge court, given the existing experience and expertise of single judge courts in Northern Ireland. I have looked at the Special Criminal Court in Ireland and have taken that into account in reaching the conclusion. Some lawyers told me that they would regard one judge as a more reliable tribunal of fact.

And he added (at paragraph 25) that 'many Diplock Court trials are heard by County Court judges. This would be appropriate under the new system proposed', until abolition in 2007.

Valuable as the opinion of the Independent Reviewer of Terrorism Legislation must be, it can only claim an absence of dissatisfaction with the Diplock system. Research into the function of Diplock Courts over a period of 30 years is vital before any endorsement of juryless trials can be made. But there must be an encouragement that, where a fair trial system is called for, there seems to be no objection to establishing a high quality of professionalism in trying criminal cases. And there is cause when examining the Northern Irish criminal jurisdiction, during troublesome times, at least to recognise that the jury system may not be the only method of ensuring a fair trial.

The existence of Diplock Courts did at least underline the principle that, at least in the case of specific crimes, a shift away from jury trial was an acceptable solution to the body politic. Consequently, there was little or no opposition to the use of Diplock Courts; indeed, the communities most directly affected by the temporary abandonment of jurors, who might have been prejudiced against this decision-making, found the shift politically acceptable. Yet not all commentators welcomed the shift away from the tradition of trial by amateurs.

The Diplock Court system was studied by Professors Jackson and Doran in 1995,[2] who made comparisons between trial by judge alone and trials by jury. The authors were not entirely complimentary at a signal for a shift of the mode of trial for serious crime. They declared in a later review[3] that they found that

> the defendant suffers an adversarial deficit in non-jury trials in at least two respects. First, jurors as the finders of factual matters (as opposed to the relevant law) could afford to take a liberal, more wide-ranging view of the prosecution evidence. Secondly, jurors were able to take a fresh perspective towards the totality of the case which professional judges who sit regularly over a period of time hearing such cases may lose sight of.

The study concluded, secondly, that a professional approach induced a certain 'case-hardening', in the sense that the judicial mind demanded a 'cooler, unemotional attitude' be taken towards the evidence.

This *soi-disant* 'adversarial deficit' is applicable in the shift away from jury trial. What they observed in the operation of Diplock Courts was general, although they did allude to a shift to a multiple (three-judge) tribunal, as is composed in the Special Criminal Court in the Republic of Ireland, the equivalent of emergency cases in the Republic.

Assuming the validity of the 'adversarial deficit' − a rash assumption that finds little empirical evidence about juries in the English system − the concept is psychologically unconvincing. Its origin smacks of an idea formulated by academic lawyers studying one very specific form of trial by judge alone. Nothing appears to be noted by the authors of the study that such a deficit (as it may have existed in the Diplock Court system) was always subject to a requirement of a reason from the single trial judge, which if adverse to the defendant is appealable, as a matter of right. The 'adversarial deficit' is conceptually reflective of a favourable trial by amateurs. It has its part to play in the debate over a mode of criminal trial that secures the individual defendant a fair trial before an independent and impartial court.

It is without doubt that the adversarial spirit that pervades the criminal trial does much to foster the forensic process of fact-finding. The mere existence of a jury of 12 citizens serves to ensure that they are the arbiters of the result. The element of populism does much to enhance the system. One almost hears the jury say (*sub silentio,*

---

[2] J Jackson and S Doran, *Judge without Jury: Diplock Trials in the Adversary System* (Oxford, Clarendon Press, 1995).
[3] (2002) *Criminal Law Review* 249 at 260.

of course): 'We are the masters here'. Everyone should read the classic work *Courts on Trial*[4] by Jerome Frank, a distinguished scholar and judge of that famous Second Circuit Court of Appeal (where Learned Hand was also a giant of a judge).

What is more significant is Frank's view of lawyers who frequently extol the jury system. In part, he said,[5] the lawyers' praise for the jury system 'stems from their vested interests in its existence'. As he says, take the jury out of a trial, and most of the drama vanishes. The criminal trial is the lawyer's artistic handiwork, the courtroom is his playhouse.

II. THE IRISH EXPERIENCE

Similar to England, Wales and Northern Ireland, juryless trials, in limited circumstances, can be heard in Ireland. The Irish situation with regard to trial by jury operates where the Executive decides that the ordinary criminal courts are inadequate to secure the effective administration of criminal justice and the preservation of public peace and good order. Article 383 of the Irish Constitution so prescribes. Part V of the Offences against the Person Act 1939 regulates the establishment and operation of the special judge-alone courts in Ireland and came into force after a government proclamation about the inadequacy of the ordinary courts, by section 35 of the 1939 Act; such proclamation has been in force since 1972. The rationale of specialist courts to remove jury trial was the incidence of juror intimidation and the potential compromising of the verdict; the justification for this move was the setting up of the Special Criminal Court in 1972, on the footing that juries were likely to be threatened by paramilitary activities. The Special Criminal Court continues to satisfy the shift to juryless trials in the cases against organised criminals, where jurors can be subject to threats and intimidation. There is also the possibility of the Director of Public Prosecutions exercising his discretion to certify for judge-alone trial where the alleged offences automatically fall within the scope of counterterrorism.

The special interest in the Irish variation to jury trial is the perceived constitutionality propounded by the devotees of populist decision-making of serious criminality. The right to equal treatment is often argued. Juryless trials, it is said, would violate Article 14 of the European

---

[4] (Princeton University Press, 1950).
[5] Ibid at 138.

Convention on Human Rights, which precludes discrimination in the enjoyment of Convention rights. Given that there is no right to a jury trial under the European Convention on Human Rights, there can be no violation of Article 14. Similarly, in Ireland the right to equal treatment is given by Article 40.1 of the Irish Constitution, although that constitutional provision does not require identical treatment of all persons without recognition of differences in some circumstances. The Irish Supreme Court has so declared.[6] Discrimination between citizens in an unjust, arbitrary, capricious or unreasonable manner *may* alone trigger the removal of jury trial; there seems to be not much wiggle-room there. An unwritten constitution is hardly likely to dissent from that sole proposition for maintaining trial by jury as a mode of criminal justice.

Assuming the validity of 'adversarial deficit' – an assumption that finds little or no empirical support – the scales of justice are better balanced if the verdict of the trial is reasoned, with the additional quality that the reasoning can be evaluated by a proper appellate system. Any 'adversarial deficit' is readily adjusted by the appellate process. And if trial by jury can be the outcome of the accused's choice, who is to deny the right to choose one's forum? It may be argued that a jury verdict which is unreasoned itself constitutes an adversarial deficit in the jury system. Is the more relaxed approach to the capacity and reliability of oral testimony (as opposed to written testimony) an adversarial deficit or a layman's flexibility?

III. TAMPERING WITH THE JURY

The affirmation by Parliament in section 44 of the Criminal Justice Act 2003 to restrict severely the application of the jury system for all serious crime was fully expounded by the Court of Appeal in June 2009 in *R v Twomey*.[7] While stoutly affirming the legislature's departure from the norm in serious criminal trials, the Court of Appeal endorsed the risk to jurors by demonstrable intimidation and confirmed the shift to a trial by judge alone. The shift became effective on the footing of two essential conditions – the evidence of jury-tampering in the jury trial, and the unexceptional conditions imposable in order to protect from

---

[6] See *O'Brien v Keogh* [1972] IR 144.
[7] *R v Twomey* [2009] EWCA Crim 1035, [2010] 1 WLR 630.

further risk. Given the two restrictions – of the real and present danger of future risk, and second, whether jury trial could properly be secured to prevent tampering – whatever evidential material had been admitted in closed and open court, trial by judge alone became acceptable. The Court of Appeal made no allusion to the different modes of trial; the shift has been readily assumed by the legislature, without more ado. The courts were concerned with the shift to juryless trial – but exceptionally.

The limited application of the trial by judge alone is emphasised by the judgment in *R v Twomey*. Lord Justice Goldring, at the outset, under the rubric of the legislative structure, states that 'in this country trial by jury is a hallowed principle of the administration of criminal justice. It is properly identified as a *right*, available to be exercised by a defendant unless and until the right is amended or circumscribed by express legislation'.[8] At the same time[9] he observed that it

> does not follow from the hallowed principle of trial by jury that trial by judge alone ... would be unfair or improperly prejudicial to the defendant. The trial would take place before an independent tribunal ... it is irrelevant whether the tribunal is judge and jury or judge alone.

This seems to countenance a trial by judge alone as equally hallowed as the collective of 12 ordinary citizens. Or does it merely point objectively to the value of juryless trials? Only in terms of any protective measures in continuing with jury trial, would it be right to consider 'an incurable compromise of the jury's objectivity'.[10]

Does it follow that any further legislative reform of trial by jury will judicially comply with the fairness demanded for all criminal trials under Article 6 of the European Convention on Human Rights? If so, it follows that the defendant should have the choice of the mode of trial on the basis that the two modes both demand a fair trial. There is no inequality in the treatment of those accused of serious crime.

[8] Ibid, para 10.
[9] Ibid, para 18.
[10] Ibid, para 19.

8

Court-craft:
Judicial and Advocate Ethics

THE AMBIENCE OF the courtroom and its participants dispensing criminal justice lies at the core of the country's power to maintain its authority of law and order. It is an institution of the state to enforce its executive powers over violations of its criminal code. The housing of the institution emphasises its majestic qualities that beckon the public to view the significance of its status. The construction of the courtroom will always need to reflect the quality of public service it emphasises; the disposition of the principal actors – the judiciary, the court's administrator, its participants in the process with their advocates and its accommodation for the vigilant populace – all demand separate treatment. To all three factors, regard is had to the architecture that reflects its function, which is unlike anything experienced elsewhere. That aspect need not deter the inquisitive or not-so-inquiring citizen; it positively does not discourage any physical presence to the important law in action; indeed it invites scrutiny from the populace in person and the media in performance of its allotted task. In short, the determination in the public forum of guilt or innocence of crime must be transparent. It attracts a critical viewpoint.

But if the surrounding circumstances call for public watchfulness, the role and function of its task, constituted to effect the will of the state, in the face of public scrutiny, needs to be understood. But does it call for some lay participation in that approach of finding the facts of crime and labelling it criminal liability? Should the composition of the fact-finder of criminality and the determiner of legal procedures on the relevant law be mixed? Should the main attribute of professionalism (in the form of qualified judges) be countered by the presence and involvement of the amateur (the unqualified juror)? These are questions that have not been fully answered in modern democracies. The Dutch provide the outstanding exception. Theirs is demonstrably a mode of criminal trial that leans exclusively on the professionalism of judges in the performance of administering the system of criminal justice. It asserts unflinchingly, to a vital element of an institution within its legal system; it is the sole determiner of civil and criminal liability, as against the vast amount of administrative justice.

Do the Dutch accurately observe the essential professionalism? There are three main aspects to the judicial process, to which I assign the label judiciality. The capacity of the amateur to participate in each one varies in ability and intensity on each stage in the process of fixing criminal liability.

The reception of the evidence is the first prerequisite. The ability to hear and understand the evidential material will vary, according to the witness's testimony and documentary material. In many cases the nature and extent of the criminal event may not be very far from the daily experience of the layman; only its effect and consequences may be less well appreciated. But in the case of other criminal activity, there may be little, if any understanding of, for example, the fraudster's habits. As I seek to explain in Chapter 10 on serious fraud trials, the nature of the criminal event is frequently so far removed from ordinary experience that the layman has inevitably to adapt his skill of appreciation to matters outside his daily exposure. That may not be significant in trials that do not involve fraudulent behaviour. But the distinction may suffice to establish a tribunal for serious fraud that encompasses professionalism of the judiciary and financial experience. Other specialist crimes may indicate specialist treatment in the mode of trial; these are issues that call for discussion in the concluding chapter.

The second stage of the criminal trial process is the evaluation and assessment of the evidential material. This, of course, always entails the evidence legally admitted by the law, and precludes any knowledge acquired other than in the courtroom. Modern experience of acquiring information from sources outside the courtroom has added complexities to the juror's oath of imbibing only what has been accepted evidentially. This factor may be insufficiently substantial so as to invalidate lay participation, even if the juror (even the judge) cannot be trusted to exclude extraneous material from the process of assessing the evidence.

It is the third aspect of the criminal trial that evokes a negative response to any lay participation. The verdict of the criminal court has to be reasoned, so that the defendant understands why the court convicts (or acquits) him or her; the monosyllabic result is insufficient to validate the process of the lay jury. Does it, however, suffice in the mixed tribunal? In essence, it can do so, if the composition of the reasoned verdict by the professional judges and the lay participants effectively spells out the ratiocination of the evidence. It is the ascertaining of the relevant arguments that leads to a probability of any effectiveness. In all systems the voting procedure that will preface any composed reasoning is strictly secret. In the French system, the judicial members do not know how the lay participants voted, and vice versa. Any sound system of a reasoned verdict cannot suffice in the absence of any knowledge in the division of the reasoned process. A reasoned verdict must be regarded as transparent. Secrecy is indivisible.

Above all there is the quality of justiciability. The ethics of the criminal trial process are also distorted in the mixed tribunal systems. One cannot escape the notion that personal attitudes to crime and its control by agents of the state are ever-present and will affect the individual's approach to criminological and penological philosophy; they constitute preconceptions to criminality. Justiciability demands the removal of these preconditions. Much of the criticism about mixed tribunals stems from the conduct of the process in the criminal court. It is important that the criminal trial exhibits the quality of fairness, of conspicuous even-handedness. Nothing dispels the criminal process more than a feeling that the trial was in some way unfair. The potential for adverse reaction to the trial is often the product of 'bias', even if the word is inappropriate in the circumstances. Social acceptance of the mode of criminal trial is often dictated by an absence or diminution of justiciability. It is at the heart of training for judgeship, whether careerist or the emanation of practical advocacy, that justiciability pervades.

It is a curiosity of our system that all questions of the disposal of the convicted defendant are decided by the judge. In this respect the jury has no direct part to play, even if at trial it might wish to influence a particular penal sanction. A criminal trial has an overriding objective of legitimating a penal sanction. But, significantly, any penal dispatch is fully articulated by the trial judge (often in the presence of the convicting jury, but with its lips sealed on any consequence of its verdict). The jury may or may not approve of the sentence the court imposes. If there really is a strong case for a lay participation in the criminal trial, the lay participants should surely have their say about the penal consequence. In the mixed tribunal systems, the jurors (including lay participants) do exercise their authority, but in the English system, juries are determinedly excluded from this stage in the process. Is there not in this instance an inconsistency in separating the two roles of trial verdict and inflicted penalty? Sentencing is treated as a professional task: not so the crucial verdict of criminality.

A not inconsiderable function in the criminal justice arena is the role of the defendant's legal representative. Incontestably, the advocate's primary function in the criminal forum is to obtain the acquittal of the client from any criminal liability, or at least some result less painful than the requisite penal sanction. There are applicable certain ethical rules which constrain the advocate's task of representing his client's best interests. The most compelling feature of the forensic process, however, is the appropriate manner of adversarial conduct that persuades the tribunal towards a favourable verdict. In that sense, the nature of the proceedings dictates the manner of persuasive advocacy, in which the mode of trial can affect the strategy of the advocate. A determinator of that strategy and the complementary factors may be its overall context of criminal combat, adversarial or inquisitorial – the ultimate goal of the trial, adversarially or inquisitorially. This differential may be only marginal; the aim of proving or disproving a case, or a simple search for the truth may, however, tend to a like result. These aims may be logically different, despite achieving the same result.

The differing aims of the advocate, however, determine the forensic duty. In the adversarial system, the aim in England to cast doubt on the burden, and in particular the standard of proof (beyond a reasonable doubt), may materially decide the method of defence, even if strictly the defendant may not embark on the contest by claiming the right to silence. But that right is now rarely resorted to, so the defendant is not obliged to ward off the arrows of attack from the evidence of the prosecution. Thus, initially, the defence counsel can negate any assumption of guilt and may rest on the presumption of innocence, even though the latter is only an evidential matter and has no implication of substantive result.

Yet, given the role of non-assistance towards an investigation of truth, the defending counsel has room for invoking the elements of doubt or assumed guilt. The English criminal trial before 12 lay jurors lends itself to an element of drama. The thespian elements of the theatre are ever-present. And before the abolition of the death penalty in 1965, the drama of the criminal trial was heightened by the sense of potential punishment in the death sentence. There is no doubt that English barristers before 1965 were given to theatrics that adorned (if that is the right word) the criminal trial. At least the attention of the print and other media took advantage of the enhanced proceedings with its tragic possibilities.

The disappearance after 1965 of this aspect of the drama of jury trial has undoubtedly altered the ethos of criminal proceedings.

The adversarial contest became less combative and less entertaining to a public seeking entertainment from jury trial. Given that change in the nature of the forensic process, one might have concluded a lessening in the dramatic qualities and a greater emphasis on the majesty of the criminal court. But was there such a lessening?

Advocacy in the criminal trial shifted in its aim. The appeal to the sober analysis of evidence and the skills of advocacy simply moved the goalposts. Ask the criminal advocate about his task and one obtained a not dissimilar answer. The advocate's prime duty was similarly to obtain his client's acquittal. The likeliest way to achieve that outcome was to employ the tactics of obscurity. The common plea was that to win over the votes of jurors meant to engage, from the outset of the trial, in throwing up in front of the jury the biggest smokescreen possible. The art of advocacy had become the art of casting doubt on the prosecution's case. Nothing in the style of addressing the jury had changed. Trial by jury retained its element of amateurism; the ability to treat the process as a search for truth remained a different exercise. It helped to bolster the claim, often made, that the jury was entitled to act perversely, contrary to the adduced evidence. Thus there grew up the assertion of the 'nullification of the jury'.

For all that is disadvantageous in the adversarial system, the inviolability of the jury's verdict of acquittal is officially sustained. It defies the rational system of a true verdict according to the evidence in the courtroom. It denies the claim, logically asserted, that the criminal trial is to be conducted by the professional judiciary.

9

Expert Evidence

E VER SINCE THE sixteenth century the courts in England have admitted as evidence the opinions of experts on matters of technology and science. In strikingly modern language, Mr Justice Saunders in 1553, in *Buckley v Rice Thomas*,[1] wrote:

> If matters arise in our law which concern other sciences or faculties we commonly apply for the aid of that science or faculty which it concerns, which is an honourable and commendable thing in our law. For thereby it appears we don't dispute all other sciences but our own, we approve of them and encourage them as things worthy of consideration.

The immediate question to the nascent common law system was how to accommodate that evidence in civil litigation. Not unnaturally, the courts turned to the testimony of eye witnesses for emulation, having deftly developed at the same time law excluding hearsay (second-hand) evidence from court deliberations. Opinions of experts were regarded as usurping the functions of the courts which rejected hearsay evidence. The judicial device was to establish an exclusionary rule that recognised that experts could give admirable evidence on matters scientific or technical which involved issues beyond the everyday knowledge of judges. What the courts did not stop to consider, let alone develop, was any intervention with the basic rules of procedure whereby the litigating parties conducted their disputes by determining what evidence each party needs to support their case, or rebut that adduced by their rival. The courts thus retained their Olympian aloofness from the forensic arena, by any system of case management or direct assistance from the expert. Throughout the centuries, experts who were merely called to express professional opinions were not witnesses, selected, instructed and paid by one or other of the parties, although the difference between the practising expert and the forensic professional was not even alluded

---

[1] *Buckley v Rice Thomas* (1554) 1 Plowden 118 at 124.

to, except in *Jones v Kaney*[2] in a separate judgment, favouring the expert witness's immunity from accusations of professional negligence, by Lord Brown of Eaton-under-Haywood. He wrote, additionally:

> Expert witnesses are to be regarded as *sui generis* in the present context. There are profound differences between them and, on the one hand, witnesses of fact; on the other hand, advocates. (For the purposes of this brief judgment I mean by an 'expert witness' a witness selected, instructed and paid by a party to litigation for his expertise and permitted on that account to give opinion evidence in the dispute. I am not referring, for example, to a treating doctor or forensic pathologist, either of whom may be called to give factual evidence in the case as well as being asked for their professional opinions upon it without their having been initially retained by either party to the dispute.)

Despite the different types of expert witness, the law did ultimately provide the courts with assessors who assisted in the understanding of scientific evidence. An omniscient legislature anticipated the need for scientific help in section 7(1) of the Senior Courts Act 1981 (based on section 98 of the Judicature Act 1925), which provides:

> In any claim of matters before it the High Court may, if it finds it fit and expedient to do so, call in the aid of one or more assessors qualified to hear and dispose of the case or matter wholly or partially with their assistance.

The Rules of the Supreme Court reflect those statutory provisions. They provide for trial by a judge with the assistance of assessors as one of the permissible modes of trial. The section in the 1981 Act made provision for the appointment in the Patent Court. In proceedings in the Admiralty Court there are special, and perhaps more fastidious, provisions. But, even given these two exceptions for allowing expertise to be involved in judging, nothing exists for the criminal jurisdictions. The jury remains unique; experts participate as ordinary witnesses. If, however, trial becomes juryless, there seems in principle nothing to prevent the expert from forming part of the panel adjudicating or acting as an assessor (or quasi-judge in the criminal trial).

---

[2] *Jones v Kaney* [2011] UKSC 13, [2011] 2 AC 398.

10

Serious Fraud Offences: Whither Their Trial?

FOR 30 YEARS the administrators of the mode of criminal trial for serious fraudsters aimed, in vain, at introducing a modification in criminal justice, supported throughout by the Labour Administration and opposed mainly by the proponents of the existing system of trial by jury as the thin end of the wedge in a culturally entrenched system of justice. The aim was concluded by a single section in the Protection of Freedom Act 2012 – section 113. Section 43 of the Criminal Justice Act 2003, notorious for its inclusion of the ill-fated IPPs (imprisonment for public protection) provided (subject to an affirmative resolution of both Houses of Parliament) for applications by the prosecution on indictment for certain fraud trials to be conducted without a jury. The 2012 Act has simply removed that section 43 from the statute book. Thus ended the protracted parliamentary episode and – seemingly for the foreseeable future – any public debate over non-jury trial for serious fraud cases. Why, and how the crusade for a modest reform to jury trial for the more serious offences was sustainably opposed is a lamentable tale of action by pressure groups and modern representative democracy. It should now become the principle that serious fraud is tried by a judge, with or without experts in financial control. But, first, the historical version of the affair in democratic rule of government.

I. WHAT CONSTITUTES FRAUD?

In *Lazarus Estates v Beasley*,[1] it was stated that

> No Court in this land will allow a person to keep an advantage he has obtained by fraud. No judgment of a court, no order of a Minister, can be

---

[1] *Lazarus Estates v Beasley* [1956] 1 QB 702, [1956] 1 All ER 341.

allowed to stand if it has been obtained by fraud. Fraud unravels everything. The court is careful not to find fraud unless it is distinctly pleaded and proved; but once it is proved it vitiates judgments, contracts and all transactions whatsoever.

Lord Parker CJ observed that fraud vitiates all transactions known to the law of however high a degree of solemnity. *Lazarus Estates* was also cited by the Supreme Court of the United Kingdom in *Prest v Petrodel Resources Ltd*.[2]

Benjamin Cardozo, in *Ultramares Corpn v Touche*,[3] said that 'fraud indicates the presence of knowledge, where knowledge does not exist'. A year earlier, in the House of Lords, Lord Buckmaster had stated that:

> Fraud is conduct which vitiates every transaction known to the law. It even vitiates a judgment of the Court. It is an insidious disease, and if clearly proved spreads to and infects the whole transaction.[4]

In his celebrated speech in *Reddaway v Banham*, Lord Macnaghten spoke of the various guises in which fraud appears in the conduct of human affairs, saying: 'fraud is infinite in variety'. A corollary, expressed by Kerr in his *Treatise on the Law of Fraud and Mistake*,[5] is that: 'The fertility of man's invention in devising new schemes of fraud is so great, that the courts have always declined to define it … reserving to themselves the liberty to deal with it under whatever form it may present itself'.

II. HISTORY

The governmental desire to bring the perpetrators of serious frauds expeditiously and effectively to book found expression in the establishment by the Lord Chancellor and the Home Secretary, Mr Douglas (later Lord) Hurd of a committee in November 1983 to examine fraud trials, under the chairmanship of Lord Roskill, a Law Lord. The Committee reported on 10 January 1986 (the report,[6] I add scholastically, lacks any index), recommending that for complex fraud cases a type of tribunal was required, as 'Fraud Trial Tribunals'. Of the eight Commissioners, there was one dissenter, Mr Walter Merricks, then secretary of the Law Society.

---

[2] *Prest v Petrodel Resources Ltd* [2013] UKSC 34, [2013] 2 AC 415.
[3] *Ultramares Corp v Touche* 255 NY 170, 174 (1931).
[4] *Jonesco v Beard* [1930] AC 298 at 301–302.
[5] 6th edn (London, Sweet & Maxwell, 1929).
[6] Roskill, *Fraud Trials Committee: Report* (London, HMSO, 1986).

In his note of dissent[7] Mr Merricks did not engage in any possible change in the existing mode of English criminal trial, but stated that 'if fundamental features as jury trials are to be reviewed, the review should be a comprehensive one not confined to a narrow band of cases of an indefinable class'; he added: 'such a fact-finding operation would, in my view, be an essential preparation for, and precondition of any initiative to modernise and reform more fundamental aspects of the trial process'. The opposition to the Roskill recommendation was substantially (not wholly) emotive. Significantly, Lord Mayhew (as Mr Patrick Mayhew, Solicitor-General in 1986) supported the Conservative Government's decision of the day, not to accept the recommendation of the Roskill Committee that serious and complex fraud trials should be tried by a special tribunal.[8] And so it became the Party's policy, as evinced in the debate in 2007 of the Fraud (Trials without a Jury) Bill, and was finally given its Parliamentary quietus on 10 May 2012 by section 113 of the Protection of Freedoms Act 2012.

Second, before I address other than emotional arguments for and against the change, it is worth a moment's pause to consider the parliamentary process, from 2003 to 2007, that thwarted the government's resolve to make the numerically significant but socially modest change. Section 43 of the Criminal Justice Act 2003 was passed through all the stages of the parliamentary process, with the *caveat* of an affirmative resolution. Despite private consultations and a seminar of interested parties that produced no indication of such an affirmative resolution, the Labour Government went ahead instead with a second reading in the Lords to implement section 43, without having the need for a further motion. The Bill received a second reading in the House of Commons by a substantial majority. At the Report stage the Government secured substantial majorities and the Bill was duly read a third time. To defy the Commons, by denying the Bill a second reading in the Lords and a Committee stage (where amendments could be debated) constituted a dangerous inroad upon the Lords' capacity to adopt such action; it was – and is – a reversal of the report of the Joint Committee on Convention which was approved by both Houses of Parliament. Significantly, that report concluded that in recent years the House of Lords will usually give a second reading to any Government Bill, 'whether based on the manifesto, or not'. As Lord Tomlinson[9] expostulated in 2007 on the

---

[7] ibid 190–99, 195 line 18.
[8] HL Deb 20 March 2007, vol 690, col 1177.
[9] ibid col 1186.

second reading in the Lords of the Fraud (Trials without a Jury) Bill, their Lordships were about to take (and nevertheless took) 'the step of voting against a second reading *at our peril*'. Perilous or not, the House of Lords flexed its lordly muscle in order to deny the Government its wish to limit jury trials. It is not without significance that section 44 of the Criminal Justice Act 2003 was not, likewise, executed. That section, which has been implemented on a few occasions since 2003, provided that the prosecution may apply for a trial to be conducted without a jury 'where there is a danger of jury tampering'.[10] The fate of section 43 deserves at least a reconsideration of the grounds for proposing an associated reform.

III. SERIOUS FRAUD OFFENCES

Quite apart from the arguments favouring the system of jury trial as the mode of a fair trial (of which there were numerous examples in the debate on 20 March 2007), two matters were advanced for advocating the change recommended by Lord Roskill and his colleagues in 1986, and repeated by Lord Justice Auld in his one-man review of the criminal courts in 2001.[11] In using a panel of experts in any frauds tribunal, Sir Robin highlighted numerous difficulties, including the precise role of expert members. Nevertheless the Government took the view that the better solution lay in section 43. It proceeded to legislate in 2007.

IV. THE 2007 DEBATE

The Attorney-General (Lord Goldsmith) was at pains to limit the scope of non-jury trials. He explained that section 43 was not a general assault on the principle of trial by jury. Nor was it about choosing between a fair trial and an unfair trial: 'it is about choosing between modes of a fair trial', and fairness required a different process in a small number of serious and complex fraud cases involving inordinately long trials with complex evidential information that became excessively burdensome for 12 jurors. Nothing has emerged in recent years to gainsay the sensible assertion that a select few cases of fraud would enhance the quality of justice if they were conducted by professionals rather

---

[10] See Lord Judge CJ in *R v Twomey* [2009] EWCA Crim 1035, [2010] 1 WLR 630.
[11] *Review of the Criminal Courts of England and Wales* (London, HMSO, 2001).

than by the cumbersome and lengthy process of trial by jury. What conceivable evidence was there (or is there) to refute this general impression gleaned by those administering the system of serious frauds? There is evidence that there are undoubtedly comparable complex cases other than in serious fraud. But does that fact invalidate the case for singling out the serious fraud trial? The answer must be that the complexities of financial transactions are peculiarly not in the experience of the average citizen, unlike other serious crimes, such as domestic violence. The composition of the mode of trial is relevant, unlike almost all other forms of criminality that come before the courts of criminal justice. The only argument surrounds the ticklish issue of admissibility. A jury is shielded from hearing certain evidence that is not excluded from trials by professionals, but that difference may need attention in investigating the process of investigation of crime, as opposed to the appropriate mode of trial. Access to information other than in the courtroom raises an issue of importance.

The most compelling – one might describe it as 'arresting' – point was in the speech by Lord Carlile of Berriew in the debate on 20 March 2007. As a Liberal Democrat peer (and at this time *not* part of any Coalition Government, but a distinct advocate of civil liberties), Lord Carlile's words are weighty, if not heavy with the expected logic of a distinguished lawyer and a past surveyor of anti-terrorist legislation. I quote his words verbatim:[12]

> I agree entirely with the noble and learned Lord that, over the years, the Diplock courts [the non-jury trials in Northern Ireland which persisted from 1972–2012] have reached high standards of justice in Northern Ireland. I also agree with him entirely that there are certain classes of case in which, in this modern age, it is no longer possible to have a reliable trial by jury, but they are a very special class of case. They are not cases where the jury has to be there for a long time or has to make a difficult judgment; they are cases where the jury system is so undermined by, for example, intimidation or threats to jurors or sectarian conflict that it is simply not possible for the jury to return a reliable verdict.

So far, so good – a model exposition of the proposed reform? This dissociation from the Diplock Courts in a tribally divided society did nothing to detract from the quality of judges, which is specifically mentioned. Similarly if the material is so complex and confusing to laymen in a jury, surely that tends to invalidate the mode of jury trial;

---

[12] HL Deb 20 March 2007, vol 690, col 1166.

it does not detract from the quality of judge alone in judicial expertise. But Lord Carlile goes on to elaborate this flawed distinction. He states – and once again I have no quarrels:

> By no stretch of the imagination do fraud cases fall into that category [presumably 'undermined ... or intimidation of jurors']. This is an attempt at a pragmatic Bill; it is an attempt by the Government to persuade the House that, quite simply, fraud cases are too burdensome for juries. However, for reasons that I shall set out, *I disagree wholeheartedly*.

If the reasons 'set out' are criminologically a matter for serious argument (pragmatic or fundamental), it can hardly result in more absolute terms of rejection. Lord Carlile, like so many of his colleagues, relies too heavily on opinion evidence, which frequently is far removed from professionalism. If the administration of the system can reasonably argue for a different, but acceptable mode of trial, what is there to negate their modest proposal that the judiciary should decide on an application which is the preferred method of an equitable system of criminal justice 'in the modern age' (which Lord Carlile rightly adheres to), and which calls for an alternative mode of trial?

But how does Lord Carlile perceive this 'modern age'? In a paragraph of his reasoning he said:[13]

> Jurors' determinations of fact are based on a collective view as lay people of the conduct of the defendant. A judge's determination of fact may in some cases – I hesitate to say this in the presence of distinguished and retired judges in this House – be sometimes idiosyncratic and a great deal worse. The annals of the law reports are full of cases where judges have made serious mistakes; as I said earlier, jurors have made few.

Whatever may be said of Lord Carlile's perception of the processes of the law, he cannot claim any empirical – let alone speculative – evidence of the decisions of jurors, unelected and unanswerable, giving monastic, monosyllabic utterances, compared with reasoned (and reviewable by way of appeal on fact and law) decisions of judges, however idiosyncratic or eccentric they may occasionally be in the civil jurisdiction. For criminal justice the jury is the inviolable determiner of fact and disregarder of law. Perversity is their option, infrequently though it is deployed. Lord Carlile's pronouncement is no more reliable than that of the mythical visitor from Mars. Indeed, academics have ingeniously constructed the concept of what they like to call 'jury nullification'!

---

[13] ibid col 1167.

If the sole criterion for testing the mode of criminal trial is the verdict of the decision-maker of the accused's guilt or innocence (a rash assumption, at the best of times), then the differential is important. But empirical evidence suggests that the differential between the judge alone and the jury system is so marginal – it is judged at 1 per cent in favour of jury acquittals – that it cannot be used as the basis for a decision on whether one mode of trial is preferred to another. If, however, the criteria are the various aspects of the criminal process (including litigant satisfaction with that process), then the differentials matter. The fact is that criminologically, we know little or nothing about the functioning of the system. The studies so far by Professor Cheryl Thomas are admirable, but they do no more than speculate that jurors behave responsibly.

V. POST-2007

It would seem politically wise not to envisage a return to section 43, although a change of administration in 2015 might influence its promoters to renew the arguments for reform. On the other hand, the composition of the upper chamber of the House of Lords might incline the law reformers not to renew the March 2007 compromise. What then? The obvious alternative is to revive the alternative of the Roskill dissenter, Mr Walter Merricks, of 30 years ago. There is now an even more pressing need for a comprehensive review 'not confined to a narrow band of an indefinable class'. Before I embark on the virtues and values of any mode of trial, there is one suggestion that addresses the 'narrow band' of serious fraud cases.

There is one persistent claim by the jury-apologists that calls for comment. Citing commentators on the system, not excluding the dramatic, and oft-quoted, remarks of Lord Devlin – 'the lamp that shows that freedom lives' – expounding the constitutional guarantees of trial by one's peers, are the claims to the citizen's right to jury trial.

In the 'battle over jury trial' – to which Lord Kingsland referred in the 2007 debate – the progenitors of the rival arguments should at least remember this: jury trial (or more specifically, the English trial by judge and jury in which the latter is the distinctive fact-finder and decision-maker) is strictly not a right at all. It is a duty upon everyone indicted before the Crown Court for a serious offence – roughly 98 per cent of all crimes. Subject to what I have to say, the defendant has no option but must subject himself to the jury's verdict – since 1967 a majority of 10 out of 12 jurors will suffice. It is at best, therefore, not a constitutional right, such as some advocates would wish, but a citizen's obligation to place his reputation before 12 good men and women who have been selected generally from among the electoral roll.

The second thing to remember is that, apart from the monarch as Head of State, there is no other public institution in our democratic system of government that is unanswerable and unaccountable for its verdicts. It pronounces its decision in monosyllables and monastically. Subject only to the consequences of a fair trial under the authority of *Taxquet v Belgium* by the Grand Chamber of the European Court of Human Rights, it is generally an acceptable mode of trial. And for the independence of the judiciary in the fairness of the mode of trial in England it has one distinctive disadvantage. The verdict of the jury is an exclusive interpretation of the result of a serious criminal offence, so long as the judge properly directs the jury. It is even more so for the appellate judge who must acknowledge the exclusive fact-finding role of the jury of 12 ordinary people. Trial by jury is an abdication of the judge's function; he may sum up the factual material, but he may not have any direct say in the jury's verdict.

The protocol of 22 March 2005, dealing with the control and management of heavy fraud cases, provided that the best handling technique for a long case is continuous management by an experienced judge nominated for the purpose. If pre-trial case management on an intensive scale is essential, what can there be against allowing a defendant at least to request trial by judge alone? The interim report of the Fraud Review Team, set up by the Attorney-General in October 2005, recommended the possibility of specialised fraud courts with specialised judges, and the final report instigated the proposed legislation of 2006/7. Choice of criminal courts has long existed for the hybrid offences whereby defendants can elect a magistrates' court or Crown Court trial. It cannot, therefore, be theoretically objectionable. Can the seriousness of criminality expel the precious element of choice? The ostensible objection is that it would be discriminatory. But all exercise of choice is just that. The only obstacle to the introduction of waiver (or Bench trial) is the fear, rational or irrational, that it would be regulated properly (by which is meant 'the thin end of the wedge' – a last-ditch plea for an indefensible argument). This is an unacceptable inroad upon the jury as the prime instrument of criminal justice. So is it time now for Lord Kingsland's plea, five and a half years ago, to 'battle over jury trial'?

This is not the place to argue for or against the present system, but to point to the criteria for choice in a rational debate (we can put on one side the utterances of pleasantries in favour of or against the jury). If the sole test is the social acceptablility of trial verdicts, the topic is unanswerable. On the basis of inadequate empirical evidence of how the jury works (or not), the difference in result between judge-alone and jury verdicts is no more than 1 per cent. Parenthetically, prosecutionally, decision-making is reserved for juries in high-profile cases. But that apart, the consensus must be that in terms of result there is at most comparability. Neither of the protagonists in the debate can claim overriding virtue for one model of fair trial rather than another – that is, if the criterion is the verdict, without more ado.

But if one reads Article 6 of European Convention on Human Rights with objectivity, the test is the quality of criminal justice that determines the mode of trial as producing a quality service, and that must involve testing the process of criminal justice, including importantly the verdict, which is decidedly not decisive. That much is the outcome of the European Court's verdict in *Taxquet*, which declined to evaluate the various modes of trial operative in the Member States of the Council of Europe. But that decision, which evaluated the evidential material requisite for admissibility at trial, did point to the issue of juristic value in the criminal trial process. Clearly, though, the constitutionality of a fair trial encompasses not just the attributes of the trial process; it includes both the investigation of criminality pre-trial and the outcome of the verdict, including the appellate process and the quality of the sentencing procedure. There is also the perception of the whole process. Does the trial induce a sense of acceptance by the prosecutor and the defendant? Does the trial inspire public confidence in the system? It is assumed by criminal practitioners that the system does evoke the public's confidence. But what evidence do we have for that supposition? I sense, impressionistically speaking, that until the Second World War the British had overwhelming faith in the jury system that was then in use. I adjudge that the support is still strong, but that there is a growing disenchantment with its validity. This is not yet sufficient to indicate a change. But, given a comprehensive review of the quality of criminal justice in the twenty-first century, we might be able to determine the future of the mode of criminal trial. I stop there to say that the need for a study of the criminal justice system in its nascent European setting appears to ripen. The two systems of the Anglo-Saxon and Continental justice systems should now be viewed in their binary, and not adversarial context. There is much to be learned from both of them in a world of mobile populaces (specifically in the growth of extradition), as the Royal Commission in 1993 under

Lord Runciman acknowledged, but felt constrained by the Commission's timetable to leave the matter for another day. That day has perhaps arrived.

The Roskill Commission of 1986 did consider the prospect of a choice by the defence (and possibly by the prosecution as well), adding an alternative tribunal of non-juries. But in the result, it opted for the nominated judge, chosen by a senior High Court judge or the Recorder of London, to choose the nature of the lay members who would be selected to sit on the Fraud Trial Tribunal. The Commission thought that trial by jury should be dispensed with only if both parties consented, and that the mode of trial should lie only with the court. And on the question of the defence alone consenting, the Commission was far from satisfied that 'many defendants would choose to be tried in this way'. Recent experience of a lack of such waiver in New South Wales and New Zealand, moreover, merely confirmed its doubts about the paucity of defendants who had so elected.

But that was 'in the early stages of our inquiry' (probably 1984–85) in the light of the experience in New South Wales (introduced in 1979 for 'long and complex cases') and in New Zealand (again in 1979, and not restricted to fraud cases). So limited an inquiry deserves to be comparatively reproduced. There appeared, moreover, to be no objection in principle to choice being elected, both by the prosecution and the defence, at the instance of ultimate decision by the court itself, whenever both parties agree. The Roskill Commission did not consider whether, if the court had to assent to the parties' 'views', the mode of trial could not be judicially negatived.

The Roskill Commission, with implicit but not specific approval, did quote a valuable instance of a jury trial by judge and lay members with relevant experience:

> Our attention was drawn to the fact that before 1978 the Director of Public Prosecutions could elect for summary trial in prosecutions under the Exchange Control Act 1947. These cases were usually heard in the City of London and went to summary trial in order to save costs and to secure a speedier result than trial by jury would allow. Magistrates in the City were considered to have a better understanding of the complexities involved. Two cases in particular were described to us as 'large revolving fund exchange control cases involving the defendants' ingenious and very complicated use of abstract and esoteric exchange control concepts.' In one of these cases the Chairman of the bench was an experienced lawyer, while the other two magistrates were a retired bank official who had worked on exchange control and a businessman with experience of the stock market

[He was Mr Kenneth Corke, an experienced liquidator]. The case took about 30 days to hear, but the lawyers estimated that it would have taken up to three or four times that length had there been trial by jury. This was mentioned to us as a practical example of the workings of a tribunal in effect consisting of a judge and two specially qualified lay members.

A judge sitting with lay members is the proposal most widely supported by those who gave evidence. Provided the lay members are well chosen, comprehension of the evidence would be at a high level. Knowledge of the background to the case, the terminology, customs and practices of the business in which the alleged fraud had been perpetrated, would be available. Provided the lay members were given an equal vote on the matter of the verdict (though not on questions of law or sentence), they could demonstrate their independence of the judge, if necessary by outvoting him. If the tribunal consists of the judge and only two lay members, the problem of assembling and maintaining a list of suitable candidates to serve would not, we think, present much difficulty.[14]

I have to confess that the Chairman of the Bench on both occasions was none other than myself. I remember it well, and have since (in 2012) explained how it came about, in a book by the Magistrates' Association on 675 years of the lay magistracy. In paragraph 8.51, at page 147, the Roskill Commission, on that evidence, concluded: 'In the light of the evidence put before us we think that a judge and two lay members would be the most appropriate tribunal to try complex fraud cases'.

The waiver issue – which essentially is the act of waiving a right – is commendably up for grabs. A prime consideration is the nature of jury trial. The protagonist of trial by jury reasserts that on a matter of serious crime (indictable, or at the sole insistence of a public prosecutor), there is the inherent obligation to criminal offences being tried by one's peers (if, only since 1967, a qualified majority of the 12 are in agreement). Strictly speaking, an obligation to undergo unequivocally (subject only to a judicial determination that there has been no abuse of the criminal prosecution in framing the case against the accused) is not a citizen's *right*. It is a duty. As such, it cannot be waived. But if it is properly (if not jurisprudentially or philosophically) regarded as a 'right', the accused must be allowed the choice of mode of trial. That much has been considered politically so in both New South Wales and New Zealand, if not also in the civilised legal world. (It exists, I think, in some jurisdictions in the USA.) (Parenthetically, it is noteworthy that

---

[14] Report (n 2) 146–47, paras 8.49 and 8.50.

Parliament has recently – in section 11 of the Defamation Act 2013 – ruled that libel cases are to be tried without a jury unless the court orders otherwise.[15])

There is, moreover, the question, raised by the Roskill Commission, that its recommendation of a Fraud Trial Tribunal would

> considerably reduce the length and cost of trials, while at the same time increasing the prospects of a sound verdict being reached. The savings of judges and court time and the greatly improved comprehension of the matters under enquiry would draw more, if not all complex fraud cases to be brought to trial and provide a further deterrent for those who seek to engage in fraudulent operations.[16]

The statement in January 2013 by the Director of Public Prosecutions, Mr (now Sir) Keir Starmer QC, of examples of invigorating pursuit of tax evaders and other fraudsters is further stimulus to such prosecutions in up-to-date charging standards – as indeed is the extended financing by the Treasury of the Serious Fraud Office. The advent of rising costs and the diminution of public funding through the legal aid scheme deserves a fresh look at the financing of public and private sources to fulfil the existing services of criminal justice. The threatened strike action by the Bar and their disinclination in December 2013 to represent eight defendants in a serious fraud trial provides a hint for a less expensive solution. I do wonder, however, whether Sir Keir was right to urge higher prison sentences for the more serious fraudulent offences. But the severity of punishment for property crimes is another subject for another debate. Custodial disposal of fraudsters is also doubtfully efficient.

VI. CONCLUSION

What next? If for the foreseeable future the prospect of trial by jury – 'an equally important component of our liberties' – is here to stay in its purest form, there is no reason to discern ways of modifying the system. And I do not stop to consider the outcome of the decision in November 2011 of the Grand Chamber of the European Court of Human

---

[15] For an early example of the legislation in action, see *Yeo v Times Newspapers* [2014] EWHC 2853 (QB), [2014] 1 WLR 971.

[16] Roskill, *Fraud Trials Committee: Report* (London, HMSO, 1986).

Rights in *Taxquet v Belgium*, the argument in favour of a waiver. We do not need to accept the recommendation in 2001 by Sir Robin Auld[17] that 'with the consent of the court ... it should be able to opt for trial by judge alone in all cases now tried on indictment ...'. Not just in serious fraud cases, but in all cases of trial by jury the defendant should be free, if the court assents, to waive the right in favour of a non-jury trial. Serious fraud offences present an opportunity to experiment, and, being essential pragmatists in good government, we should give the idea a trial.

---

[17] Review (n 7) 181, section 118.

11

Waiver or Choice: An Australasian Example

THERE IS NO doubt that jury service includes a duty on the individual juror to perform the responsibility of a civil obligation. Even in the case of some lengthy trials, which are becoming more a feature of criminal justice, the onerousness of the task may be viewed with acceptance, even with a sense of duty. In April 1963 the Morris Departmental Committee on Jury Service concluded that, while jury service was regarded as a civic duty, it had no desire to pronounce on whether jury trial was a right – or even a fundamental freedom! While public opinion today may not be so fulsome in its eulogy of the system, this dispute still stands. Is the system a right that the defendant possesses? Or is it more easily considered as an obligation for the defendant to undergo? The answer is not insignificant. If trial by jury is an accused's right, then logically he should be able to waive his right in favour of an alternative mode of trial. To those who assert that it is a right, it is more important to notice that every citizen has a constitutional guarantee of a fair trial by an independent and impartial court. If the tribunal acceptably includes lay participation, is that system fair as the normal mode of trial? The jurisprudence of the European Court of Human Rights would appear to endorse trial by jury as a mode of trial under Article 6 of the Convention.

Even when the system is referred to as establishing a right, there is confusion in the nomenclature. When society enacts the precise mode of trial, it expresses the apt title. Since all but the most serious crimes are dealt with by magistrates in summary trial, a case can only be suitably sent to the Crown Court for jury trial if the magistrate agrees.

This confusion deserves a clarion call for greater clarity in the delineation of procedural rights, at whatever level the criminal offence is pitched. Would it not be better that any option of jury trial should be matched with the alternative of trial by judge alone? In short, ought there to be a waiver of jury trial, in favour of judge alone?

The concept of a waiver to trial by jury in the UK is absent from much debate, although increasingly it is being accepted by other jurisdictions which employ jury trial for serious criminal cases. Some of the state courts in America and in the main countries of the Commonwealth – particularly Australia, New Zealand and Canada – have introduced the waiver system in various forms, which are not discussed here. Instead, there is a debate on the use of a juryless option. In the literature, there are four lines of argument that suggest maintaining the present absence of any waiver. First, it is claimed that any option would undermine the institution of jury trial. Second, any option would seem to run against the criminal justice culture and long-held traditions of jury trial. This argument is a blown-up version of the first – a grander concept of society's view of juries. The third charge might not be readily receptive to the judiciary which under the jury system accepts the decision of guilt or innocence. Fourth, the accused should not have control over society's declaration on the mode of trial. The general option to a judge-alone trial is manifestly to follow the movement of most European democracies to accept lay participation in other systems – in short, a mixture of judges and lay persons.

Without a full-scale debate on the appropriate reasoning for jury trial, it must be conceded that jury trial should be seen not merely as a means of ensuring public confidence, but also as a protection to defendants, to warrant it being regarded as a 'right'. It follows that defendants should then be entitled to waive such a 'right' when they assert, for whatever reason, that it may not in an individual case work to their benefit, subject possibly to circumstances in which the prosecution or the court should be free to oppose the defendant's opinion, which is one of the matters to be addressed in considering how a system of waiver ought to operate in practice. Waiver could properly be described as a right for the defendant to choose how his fate should be determined.

Since the potential sanction facing the defendant is severe enough – whether imprisonment or a monetary penalty – it seems sensible to allow the defendant to assess the consequence. Any objection that the accused should not have full control over the decision on the mode of trial, or any waiver system, should always be ultimately a decision of the court. Waiver of a right should come under court management. Likewise a choice of mode of trial should be qualified by the judiciary. If choice is permissible by the defendant, it is axiomatic that he or she cannot select the judge who will try the case, unless of course the defendant was able to seek the judge's recusal on the ground of bias.

The time is ripe to consider jury waiver or defendant choice as options for reform in the modernisation of criminal justice. Against the background of increasing public demand for judges to become more directly involved in the trial process, whether as decision-makers or in mixed tribunals, it is appropriate that the inherent responsibility of a judge for the decision of guilt or innocence should be officially endorsed.

The second reason would be the official recognition in the statute that the credibility and reliability of witnesses, the conduct of the trial process and the control of the advocates (both prosecution and defence counsel) should always remain the responsibility of the court. Without labouring the point of the dramatic elements of the courtroom, a criminal trial should preserve the authority and dignity of sober adjudication. A forensic process should evoke the public majesty of the institution. Any lay participation in the mode of trial is helpfully susceptible to human experience. Equally, though, it can be disadvantageous through influences such as social media or human interaction outwith, and out of reach of, the courtroom and any judicial authority. The Dutch insistence on a criminal trial being exclusively the administration of justice as part of the legal system is unanswerable. It recognises no direct public intrusion; only the scrutiny of openness and surveillance by the demands of vigilance. Its effectiveness is judged by the strength of reasoned verdicts at trial.

Criminal justice can no longer be the resolution of a dispute between rivals in a game. The sporting analogy misses the target; it is not a question of scoring points, or of declaring the winner and loser. The public demand for the search for the truth behind the criminal event asks for nothing less than the search for a true verdict. It should never contemplate a miscarriage of justice, an unequal result. A criminal trial is a serious venture in maintaining society's relationship to its citizenry, in the pursuit of peace, order and good government.

When the late Lord Bingham enumerated the eight principles of the classic book on *The Rule of Law*,[1] he might have given the system of jury trial as an example of the seventh principle, that 'adjudicative procedure provided by the State should be fair'. The specific example of opting for one's mode of trial has now been endorsed by the Court of Appeal. In *R (Howard League for Penal Reform and Prisoner Advice Service) v The Lord Chancellor*[2] it was held that systems of official

---

[1] (Penguin, 2011) 90.

[2] *R (Howard League for Penal Reform and Prisoner Advice Service) v The Lord Chancellor* [2014] EWCA Civ 244, [2017] 4 WLR 92.

decision-making – in this case the system of legal aid – must be intrinsically capable of delivering a fair outcome in every case. So too, trial by jury, whether it imposes a duty on or grants a right to the offender, in essence imports a choice or waiver in favour of juryless trial.

This overriding principle of fairness in systemic adjudication (fairness in the system) in jury trial has long been advocated; yet not until now is it demonstrably accepted in modern society. Hitherto, Article 6 of the European Convention on Human Rights, embodied into English law in the Human Rights Act 1998, guarantees every person charged with a criminal offence a fair hearing before an independent and impartial tribunal, but it omits to indicate what the precise mode of trial should be. That was left undecided by the Grand Chamber of the European Court of Human Rights in the case of *Taxquet v Belgium* in November 2010, but there is nothing left for the municipal court to provide that a fair trial involves a choice or waiver of the mode of trial. Many of the older Commonwealth jurisdictions have introduced into their law specific provisions that permit accused persons to choose or waive alternatives to jury trial.

In the Court of Appeal case, specialist prison law and public law, combined with the Legal Aid Agency to deliver publicly-funded legal services for prisoners, sufficed as systemic fairness. What constitutes systemic fairness in the case of those facing jury trial? Surely the seriousness of jury trial also suffices.

I. AN AUSTRALASIAN EXAMPLE

For several years now, various jurisdictions in parts of the old Commonwealth have adopted precedents for alternative options to trial by jury. I describe, as a helpful guidance, sections 132 and 132A of the New South Wales Criminal Procedure Act 1986 introducing trial by judge alone in criminal proceedings.

Section 132 provides that if the accused person agrees to a trial by judge alone, the court must make such a trial, but if the accused does not apply, the court is not bound to order trial by judge alone. If the prosecutor does not support the application, the court has a discretion to make a trial by judge alone 'if it considers that it is in the interest of justice to do so'. And the court may refuse a trial by judge alone if it considers that the trial would involve a factual issue that requires the application of community standards (including issues of reasonableness, negligence, indecency, obscenity or dangerousness). But trial by judge alone cannot be made unless the accused has sought and received advice on juryless trial from a practising lawyer.

This provision is thus more than a waiver or a choice to undergo a trial by judge alone. It gives the accused person the right to insist on trial by judge alone, as Bentham described the attitude in 1792. The right may be qualified by the prosecutor but only if the court considers it in the interests of justice to make the order. The offender and prosecutor are additionally allowed to apply for an order for trial by judge alone to be replaced by jury trial before the date fixed for trial.

In *R v King* and *R v Dean* in 2013[3] the Court of Appeal held that a judge, in determining an application for trial by judge alone, should not take into account that a jury is better able to determine issues of credibility than a judge. The absence of substantial, past adverse media publicity about the accused is frequently raised. But the courts have considered that the discretion to reject evidence where its probative value is (or may be) outweighed by its prejudicial effect has little, if any, role to play in judge-alone trial.

Section 133 is important in directing the outcome of the trial by judge alone. A judge trying a case alone may make any finding that could have been made by a jury on the verdict of the guilt of the accused. Any such finding has the same effect as a jury verdict. The judge alone is required to state the relevant principles of law that he applies and the findings of fact upon which the judge relied. The judge is further required to take into account any warning that would be given to a jury.

The elaborate procedure implicitly rejects a common objection by proponents of jury trial that an accused ought not to have a full measure of control over the mode of trial. The suggestion is, however, not that defendants should always, as a matter of principle, be entitled to absolute control. The argument rests perversely on whether jury trial is a 'right'. But if jury trial is not a right, but a duty, waiver does not arise. The question is whether the accused thinks that he will have a fair trial. He is the judge of his fate in criminal proceedings.

---

[3] *R v King* [2013] NSWSC 448; *R v Dean* [2013] NSWSC 661.

12

Jury Reality: The Search for Empirical Evidence

H ISTORICALLY, CRIMINAL OFFENDERS in England were tried publicly by their peers, a system regarded as an essential element of a fair and just model of criminal justice. Trial by jury has persisted in the Anglo-Saxon systems exclusively only for a small number of serious offences, while many other countries provide for various forms of lay participation alongside professional judges, where mixed tribunals render their joint verdict.

Both systems focus on the principle that the involvement of lay participation provides a valuable safeguard to civil liberties (terminologically, human rights). The employment of jurors, whether or not selected from the electoral roll, to adjudicate on disputes is based on an overwhelming priority of individual freedom from governmental control. Others give the layman an equal say in the process. At least until the Enlightenment in the late seventeenth century, the jury continued to be highly valued and also criticised for its involvement whenever the ordinary citizen became involved in the legal system. But there is in modern democracies a nascent feeling of uncertainty about the function of the jury system in a society that is distinctly more complex, scientifically and technologically. That lack of certainty about the system is inherently difficult to test, simply because of the legal restriction preventing researchers from invading the jury room and interviewing individual jurors.

Resort to alternative tests has thus been applied. Mock trials are the main resort of jury research, the latest of which comes from the pellucid pen of a doctoral researcher at the University of Huddersfield.[1]

---

[1] D Willmott, 'An Examination of the Relationship between Juror Attitudes, Psychological Constructs, and Verdict Decisions within Rape Trials' (Doctoral thesis, University of Huddersfield, 2018).

Dr Dominic Willmott focuses our attention on the extent to which psychological constructs, attitudes and characteristics of jurors infect the decision-making process, from the reception of material (often today more conflicting and confusing) to the moment of deliberation on the verdict. His study, which re-enacted rape trials to live audiences of mock jurors and suggests that there are implications for other subjects on trial, is also disturbing. Myths persisted in other criminal cases. Whilst previous research has concluded on the examination of jury verdicts, in isolation from the process, the Huddersfield study focused on psychological personality traits of jurors, and reveals in-built preconceptions and prejudices of individual jurors that persist throughout the trial process. In short, this unique methodological study elucidating empirical evidence of jury habits evokes a conclusion that trials are susceptibly less than fair. Miscarriages of justice are alarmingly terrible.

History tells us little of use about past juries. Whatever we have been able to glean from how juries function, the picture is gravely distorted by the absence of direct evidence from the jury, or even indirectly by remote studies of juries via mock trials. Misguidedly, we depend on the powerful instinct of our personal experiences of the system.

Devoid of hard data, we resort to that emotional tool of human experience and dubious tales from isolated cases. Legal professional attitudes to the jury depend on the disputatious environment and lawyer's disposition to the scene of his professional obligations. Advocacy in front of the jury depends on such variables as the nature of the criminal event under investigation and the composition of the jurors to be addressed. Jury advocates unwittingly depend on their intuition. As Bertrand Russell observed back in the 1940s, belief dies hard.

Despite these handicaps, there is good cause to study and assess what little reason does exist. It is far from being irrelevant. It nevertheless deserves assessment: two basic components are relevant. First, what conclusion should we draw from the understanding of the evidential material, assuming, as one might, that the jury adheres faithfully to its oath and to the judicial direction on the law? To that extent the model insists upon a degree of professionalism in its imposition of the relevant law. Jurors are not in any meaningful sense the arbiters of the law. Second, assuming the requisite standard of reception of the relevant evidence (assuming that nothing is gained from sources that are inadmissible), what can be considered by the jury in its deliberation of the verdict? It is at this point that there is a factor that can validate the verdict. The most compelling ground for the legitimate (applying the law) validity of the verdict is the reasoning process, the ratiocination of the verdict. Nothing in the process of decision-making satisfies this basic requirement more than the clarity and certainty of the reasons given for arriving at the result, which forensically calls for a finding of certainty that precludes any reasonable doubt – the standard of proof that calls for a certainty beyond an ordinary daily event; the nature of proof that exceeds beyond belief.

Apropos the first element, it would be foolish to deny that the juror's understanding of the evidence, both oral and written, is significantly different from the other actors in the trial process who are trained and qualified in the assessment of the credibility and reliability of the witness. The layman is as susceptible of evaluating evidence as is the judicial or professional person. It is, however, at this point where doubt arises. Given the development of modern technology and science – DNA is one example – the evidence inevitably speaks primarily to the technologist or the scientist. One of the advocate's prime examples is the gulf between the thought-process of the scientist and of the lawyer, if only because the former treats the subject-matter as inconclusive fact, whereas the lawyer requires finality of the question, the more so if trained under a system that is devoted to procedure. It should be observed that there is a point of departure here, where the lawyer in western Europe proceeds ideologically (empirically) on the approach to statutory (core) provisions. Here, there is positive evidence of a different meaning of the legal provision and its factual reliance today.

If the evidential material in the criminal court demonstrates a knowledge outside ordinary experience, in that it requires expert testimony to explain it to the novice adjudicator, the question arises about how to overcome the gulf. The most compelling argument in favour of lay participation in harmony or tandem with the judiciary is that of Hegel in his concept of the Philosophy of Right, which acknowledges the prejudice of everyone in their everyday life. If justice is manifestly seen to be done, the tribunal that lacks any lay participation could not properly be considered to impart the true nature of any criminal event. This is because if lay people are excluded from the process, the court becomes the arena of professional lawyers, dictating the forensic process in all its forms; however well-meaning, they aim to administer justice in a manner and a language that the public cannot be expected to understand. The legal process may be frustrated if they require explanation to non-professionals. That is the primary function of a vigilant press.

The proposition as an important safeguard is a truism. But it depends for its validity on the notion of populism; if invoked, it imposes a dominance of amateurism over the training and skill of the qualified lawyer. It must find its effect in ensuring that the professional institution is regulated by the law with a full appellate system, also by a monitoring and surveillance of the judiciary and professional lawyers.

It is worth stating, as Jerome Frank once pithily wrote, that all of us are subject to pre-condition at birth and by the socialising process of family, as well as, educationally, by the state. What is significant is that our prejudices, too often expressed or inflicted unexpressed, are specifically suppressed by professional training. That is what is regarded as accuracy and transparency, more of which are rightly called upon as a prerequisite of the decision-maker. If the professional tribunal fails to observe the tenets and ethics of its professional obligations, then public justice suffers and needs to be corrected. That is why the legal system establishes, jurisprudentially, the principle of abuse of process. The giving of reasons for a verdict provides a means of testing the reliability of the ratiocination. It is unavailable with the unreasoned verdict; at best, the jury's monosyllabic utterance is guesswork. One has to observe that, in that absence, the commentator reaches for the so-called principle of nullification.

In the absence of empirical evidence about prejudicial attitudes that are unspoken and imitative, it may be assumed that impartiality in the decision-maker is indiscriminately applied. But it is precisely because there is always the danger of prejudice, that our system goes to such lengths to perform what I like to call justiciability – that is to display the virtues and values of impartial treatment to all-comers.

Dr Willmott's prescription suggests three possible solutions: the first is to train all jurors in rape trials about the possibility of bias; his second alternative would see prospective jurors being screened and determined to be eligible before hearing rape trials (with the possibility of applying jury screening only in such cases where the strength of the prospective bias and the lack of corroborative evidence might see a need for juror bias to be reduced in order to comply with the right to a fair trial). No doubt surveillance and monitoring might counter the misimplementation of jury verdicts. Judges nowadays are routinely warning jurors of the dangers of indulging their prejudices. But the degree to which jurors can put aside their innate feelings and give a true verdict on the evidence admitted in the courtroom, and the degree of self-discipline which can be imposed, means that effective remedies must be sought.

The notion of juror screening asserted as part of a *voir-dire* process, the basis of Dr Willmott's study, may seem a sensible proposal. That would follow the US experience of quizzing the expectant jurors.

It would mean, at the very least, a revival of the peremptory challenges or questioning whether jurors were genuinely fit for jury service; it would call for a distinct shift in jury selection. (Peremptory challenges were abolished in England and Wales by the Criminal Justice Act 1988.) But the results of this research, and the disturbing levels of bias they expose, lead to the third possibility for reform: the replacement of juries in rape trials by a judge sitting alone. Until research conducted by scholars can unveil the secrecy of jury deliberation, the results from studies can achieve little or no policy change. It seems, however, that the results of Dr Willmott's research are being taken seriously by those responsible for the administration of justice in England and Wales, and, at the time of writing, discussions are taking place with a view to extending the scope of the research and examine the possibility of real policy change.

13

The Scope of Jury Trial and Reasoned Decisions

THE OBLIGATION (duty or right) of the citizen to undergo trial by jury in *all* serious criminal offences always depended upon the social acceptability of the concept of trial by one's peers, today an Anglo-American style of modern criminal justice. Whatever social underpinning sustained its historical origins, there has been an undoubted support of the public for equating jury trial unqualifiedly with serious crime. A response to any contemporary reform has been met dominantly by a resistance to any public change. This popularity has waned insufficiently under minor changes, but not until the Worboys case in January 2018 were decisions made publicly in the administration of justice that questioned seriously the public's growing demand for greater transparency in criminal justice. It came with the revelation that the release from prison, decided by the Parole Board, had not been publicly communicated.

John Worboys, a black cab driver, was convicted in 2009 at Croydon Crown Court of 19 offences against 12 women, one of whom was raped and five sexually assaulted.[1] The police believed that Worboys had attacked hundreds more, and were investigating, although politicians, lawyers, other victims and women's groups reacted volubly to the scale of Worboys' criminality.

Worboys was sentenced to the minimum term of eight years' imprisonment, subject to an indeterminate sentence for public protection (IPPs were introduced into the legislation in 2003, but prospectively abolished in 2012). He sought his discharge from prison soon after he had served the requisite term of the determinate sentence. The power to discharge Worboys under the IPP imprisonment became the function of the Parole Board, who had to determine whether he continued to present a risk of further danger. The Parole Board's decision alone determined the release of the prisoner.

---

[1] *Worboys* (2009) Croydon Crown Ct.

Since 2011, the rules of the Parole Board have imposed on the panel deciding the case the duty to give written reasons for their decision; the reasons have to be given, signed by the chair of the panel. Where there is a duty to give reasons for any decision made during the course of hearing an application for release, they are required to be adequate and intelligible. The courts have laid down that the reasons must focus on the question of risk, so that the Board should identify in broad terms whether the matter judged in the Board's view is pointing towards or against a continuing risk of offending, and the Board's reasoning for striking the balancing act. That requires that the panel, in its letter on the decision, should summarise the considerations which had in fact led to the final decision. No standard was set for the letter; the courts did not require elaborate or impeccable standards of draftsmanship. Reasons had to be reasonably supplied, but no more. Helpfully, the Board has issued its own guidance on the draftsmanship. This suggests that the decision should be divided into sections indicating an analysis of the prisoner's offending, the identifiable risk factors, evidence that the prisoner has changed during the sentence, an assessment of how the prisoner has changed, plus an assessment of the risk of reoffending and of serious harm, as well as plans to manage that risk. The guidance emphasises that the panel's conclusions on all those issues, and its decision should be clearly stated.

The letter setting out the summary of the issues is sent only to the prisoner, the relevant probation service, the prison service and to the Secretary of State. Unless the prisoner decides to circulate the letter, there is no wider dissemination of the Parole Board's decision. It is manifest from the reaction of the chairman of the Board, Professor Nicholas Hawkins, that the clamour for greater transparency means that the claims of the public for better knowledge about the prospective release of such prisoners is likely to be considered. The clamour comes partly from the victims of the prisoner, whether that particular victim was involved in the criminal proceedings.

The significance of the Worboys case is the extent of information supplied by the administration of the penal system. The Supreme Court, in 2013, considered that the case of a prisoner serving a sentence of imprisonment for public protection (IPP) was exactly the same as for any other indeterminate sentence. The prisoner argued that, as the statutory pre-condition for the imposition of the IPP sentence was the existence of a significant risk of serious harm, only such a risk could justify a detention of longer than the minimum term. The Supreme Court rejected that contention. It considered that the rules of the sentencing court and the powers of the Parole Board were equally applicable. It is this difference in treating the IPP prisoner as a special class of persons to be denied further discharge that is now to be considered separately, and more restrictively. That penological approach does not impinge on the view that the Worboys case has demonstrated the public's view about decision-making, but it is arguable that it does demonstrate the public view about that part of the criminal justice system that deals with the prisoner whose maldeeds uniquely demonstrate a plea for the special detention powers relating to dangerous offenders. It also indicates a much greater intolerance of dangerous offenders, and greater tolerance towards other serious offenders who are subject to jury trial. If I am right in thinking that public support for trial by jury goes much too widely against the serious offender who does not present any risk factors of serious harm, then there is every reason for making trial by jury applicable only in IPP offences, such as was explained in the setting up of Diplock Courts in Northern Ireland against terrorists who had killed indiscriminately. The public confidence in jury trial needs re-assessment in its blanket coverage of all serious offenders.

14

Perverse Verdicts: Jury Nullification

THERE IS A widespread consensus among academic writers on the law that jury nullification can be regarded as compatible with the Rule of Law. Not surprisingly, there is no support from the judiciary for the concept. But there is a general public awareness that some verdicts by juries are simply unreasonable, according to the standards of decision-making in criminal trials, and should not be allowed to stand; they simply detract from the juror's oath to act upon admissible evidence in court. Any assessment of the policy of the law and its instant application is strictly irrelevant to the jury's verdict.

If a jury acquits an offender, there is, generally speaking, nothing to be done. The unreasoned verdict of innocence is inviolate, and beyond the reach of any appellate system. If, however, the verdict is one of guilt, but is thought to have been contrary to the law and evidence in the case, the appellate system should ordinarily provide the remedy and reverse the perverse verdict. Thus, unequal treatment towards verdicts of guilt or of innocence provides a singular problem. Should the inviolate verdict be reversed on the grounds that perversity should not be allowed to stand?

The problem is, however, not so easily resolved, whether the perversity relates to a rejection or dismissal of the law, or is simply an improper assessment of the material evidence adduced in the courtroom – which is the statutory function of jurors under the jury oath. Since the application of the law is a matter exclusively for the judge to declare and for the jury to act upon, there appears to be ample justification for judicial intervention in the decision-making. Even then the task of establishing the perversity may not be so apparent.

I previously experienced a case where the problem arose. In the early 1970s a number of individuals, who were acolytes of Ms Pat Arrowsmith, strongly objected to British troops serving in Northern Ireland as part of the British Army which was sent to the Province in December 1969 in aid of the civil power, as the Royal Ulster Constabulary appeared to be failing effectively to maintain law and order in the Province. Eleven of Pat Arrowsmith's associates were arrested in the town of Aldershot, distributing leaflets to the soldiers in the town who might be destined to serve in Northern Ireland. They were indisputably in breach of the criminal law. The Incitement to Disaffection Act 1934, enacted at the time of the Fascist riots of the 1930s in London, clearly declared such conduct as a breach of the law, introduced to deal with troubles in the streets of England. They were duly prosecuted in a trial at the Old Bailey, during which overwhelming evidence was adduced, examined, and cross-examined by counsel for the eleven.

It was made clear to defence counsel at the conclusion of the acquittal, after 51 days of trial, of all eleven defendants that the jury had expressed among themselves after only five days of the evidence that they were never going to find any of the defendants guilty of any offence. Nearly five weeks later, they were all acquitted. Jurors who were keen to communicate their rejection of the prosecution's case did so for different reasons. A few of the more ardent supporters of the leafleters disliked the legislation passed by Parliament in 1934. Most jurors, however, did not dispute the validity of the law, but were insistent that the defendants in post-war Britain were not beholden to a law that prevailed during the Fascist riots of the 1930s. The law was clearly inappropriate to the case of persuading peacetime members of the armed forces. Other jurors, who were not averse to the 1934 Act, however, disregarded the evidence of leafleting as an act of incitement; they felt that the defendants should be allowed to engage in the activity of distributing the leaflets.

Was the jurors' rejective action against the law, or at least against its application in 1972 breaking the prescribed law? If, technically, the eleven were committing a criminal act, the jury was unwilling to say so in its verdict. They deliberately nullified the law that had been directed by the trial judge.

Any nullification of a jury verdict on the grounds that the jurors had acted against the law might be an acceptable social solution, if the jury system contains, impliedly, a function of negativing a statutory provision as part of a democratic process – a kind of 'mini-Parliament' as depicted in Lord Devlin's notion of the jury. Some, but not this author, would praise the enlightened view of a very distinguished judge. Others would utter the phrase of Professor Penny Darbyshire who declared that Lord Devlin's 'lamp that shows that freedom lives' is not worth a candle!

If, on the other hand, a judge's verdict of the jury is clearly a conclusion of the assessment that the evidence is unreasonable, the issue is more clear-cut. Fact-finding is for the jury, influenced but no more than persuaded by the judicial summing-up. That is the juror's prerogative. It is a judgment that is personal to each juror to affect his or her oath, with the caveat that, since 1974, the verdict can, after more than two hours' deliberations, be given by the majority; otherwise unanimity is required. There seems to be little room for judicial or other intervention into a jury's verdict on the finding of fact. The acquittal remains a mysterious part of an oracular system that indulges in fair play in a contested dispute between the citizen and the state. There is no nullification of a jury's acquittal, however misapplied. Lord Goddard, a scholarly and conservative Lord Chief Justice, once observed extra-judicially that 'no-one has yet been able to find a way [except to propose its abolition] of depriving a British jury of its privilege of returning a perverse verdict'.[1]

In his Review of the Criminal Courts in 2001, Sir Robin Auld recommended a reform of perverse verdicts. His plea was rejected by the Government, and none has been hinted at since. Perversity prevails as part of the system.

---

[1] HL Deb December 1985, vol 191.

15

The Magistracy Today: Towards Professionalism

O F ALL THE criminal trials that take place in the magistrates' courts of England and Wales (which constitute 95 per cent of all trials in the criminal courts), less than 10 per cent are tried by individual District Judges (formerly stipendiary magistrates), of whom, in 2018, there were about 150 lawyers sitting full-time and 150 lawyers sitting part-time. As professional lawyers aspiring to judicial preferment, they are recruited and trained separately; they are culturally distinct from the 15,000 or so lay magistrates who sit in panels of three to try the 95 per cent of less-serious criminal cases. But the proportion of District Judges and lay magistrates is growing steadily. Generally speaking, there are no mixed criminal tribunals for adult offenders, composed of District Judges and lay magistrates. Justices of the Peace (to give the lay magistrates their ancient title) are drawn from all walks of life, with little or no qualification in the processes of judicial behaviour. Nevertheless, by virtue of initial training and in-service tuition, many of them readily exhibit professionalism in their separate fields of endeavour. Sitting as a magistrate, therefore, is distinct from any system of lay participation alongside the qualified judiciary. Moreover, they are required to sit magisterialy for at least 26 days a year. Significantly, they acquire the habits of judiciality. Yet there is no formal judicial disparity between the Justice of the Peace and the District Judge.

Although not disqualified from appointment to the lay bench of the magistracy, lawyers are an uncommon sight among those sitting in judgment. Even those lawyers engaged in legal practice (including conceivably a Queen's Counsel, no less) may exceptionally be appointed; the only restriction is that they cannot appear as counsel in the courts where they might be asked to sit. That such a legally qualified magistrate might find himself or herself exceptionally adjudicating on a case conducted by a fellow practitioner could be avoided by instant disqualification from sitting. The odd occasion in which a legal practitioner would be one of three magistrates seems rarely to have aroused public (let alone specialist) interest; a suggestion for emulation on a regular basis has gone unheard, even unnoticed beyond the instant case.

But that was then – the 1970s. Experience, however, indicated a potential widening of the appointment of Justices of the Peace, as well as a growing tendency to appoint legally qualified persons as stipendiary magistrates. When I came to the Bar, there was barely a handful of legal practitioners among the company of stipendiary magistrates. At that time the experiment was largely confined to metropolitan districts outside central London. The position now of at least 150 District Judges in and out of London is remarkably different. It suggests a further development of qualified lawyers, while the system remains predominantly composed of selected candidates who display talents for adjudicating criminal cases on less serious offences and reflect a diversity in age and sex. They are distinctly not jurors, although they may seem to be quasi-judges. Although are they expected to state the reasons for their verdict, the nature of the criminal event hardly extends the magistracy from ticking boxes, rather than handing down a reasoned judgment. The traditional limitation of a magistrate's power to include imprisonment (at present a maximum six months' sentence) is distinct from the juror who has no direct effect on the question of sentencing, custodial or non-custodial. Although there has been talk of increasing the power of imprisonment, the Prisons and Courts Bill (still in embryo and unlikely to be enacted) contains no provision with regard to sentencing. The jury is exclusively the fact-finding aspect of a criminal trial. Magistrates are constantly alive to the existence of the capacity to intervene by ordering imprisonment in the wide range of offences tried in the magistrates' court. Moreover, magistrates experience the courts' policy of sentencing. In the limited scope of appeals against the sentence of a magistrates' court, the magistrate will sit alongside the judge at the Crown Court. It may not remain so exceptional, since official statements frequently indicate that there are serious proposals to extend the power of imprisonment to 12 months. If so, there will be increasing use by magistrates of the new power at their disposal.

Apart from participation in the sentencing of the court in lesser crimes, there is little doubt that the magistracy does affect, to a considerable extent, the large prison population of 83,000 prisoners on an average daily basis. Reducing this is a factor in its future use by the criminal justice systems overall. Given the primary function of fact-finding and other ancillary matters pertaining to the remand of offenders pending trial (including bail actions) there is nevertheless a quality of criminal justice by the magistracy that is perceived by public opinion. Here there is grow-ing evidence of the association of the District Judge and the Justice of the Peace impacting on the quality of justice administered. There is no obstacle to a mixed tribunal of District Judge and Justice of the Peace. Their occasional use in the past may be replicated whenever, increas-ingly, there are complex issues at stake. I can give two examples that I experienced in 1981. I sat as the chairman (magistrate) in both cases, with two colleagues who brought valuable expertise to the problem. The two cases involved the Exchange Control Act 1947 (dissolved shortly afterwards), and what were called floating frauds, the defendants organ-ising the movement of money across the world, in the course of which they handsomely picked up the floating dollar premium.

My colleagues were the international director of Barclays Bank, a global expert in financial transactions, and the chairman of the Royal Opera House, who was an outstanding expert of international fame. Both demonstrated wide understanding of international finance and imbued the sense of adjudication in the world of serious fraud. For 30 days we sat and heard the argument, forensically conducted. We reserved our judgment and delivered it a few weeks later – all 30 pages – convicted the two stockbrokers, and fined them heavily. I recall our excellent justices' clerk expressing surprise at the idea of a reasoned judgment: it was an open invitation, he said, to an appeal. The stockbrokers did not appeal. Our experience was commended by the Roskill Committee on Serious Frauds in 1986; its recommendation for these trials to be heard by judge alone or with experts remains unim-plemented, despite serious attempts to legislate for specialist trials. The trend in the mode of trial in criminal justice is towards greater professionalism, despite the favouring of trial by jury in serious cases.

16

Jury Trial – A Modern
Mode of Trial

A COLLECTION OF 12 good men and true has historically been the renowned system for a fair trial for serious crime. It has been characterised throughout its long history as at least conspicuously even-handed between the state and its citizenry; the more so, in recent times. The burden of proof always rests on the prosecution. Even if trial by jury became democratic only in 1972 (until then only property-owners qualified for jury service) and fully representative of the country's citizenry after 2003, jury trial uniquely respected the trend of lay participation alongside the judiciary. But the uniqueness of the jury system was always predicated on safeguards for the protection to which the accused was afforded in law, and held that a prisoner, for the first time after he became eligible in 1898 as a witness in his defence, was emphatically presumed to be factually innocent. The right not to give evidence in his own trial was indicative of the accused's position of putting the burden of proof squarely on the state. The accused's right not to assist in the prosecution's duty to prove its case was an affirmation of the adversarial system of trial; it added nothing by way of assistance to finding the truth of the event. The lack of inference that could be drawn from the defendant's silence reinforced the claim often made that the English adversarial system of jury trial is a game and not a search for the truth.

The position of a defendant in a criminal trial having his options open to him in relation to giving evidence has notionally changed since the defendant could give evidence under the legislation of 1898; none more so than the inferences which a jury could draw from the accused wishing not to exercise his right to give evidence. This changed in a fasciculus of sections in the Criminal Justice and Public Order Act 1994. Although the new law on the drawing of inferences from the accused's silence predictably did not shorten the trial, there is, a quarter of a century later, no good reason to detect a change in the length of jury trial. There is much evidence that the decision of an accused to sit back and see whether the prosecution proves its case is less prominent. Only for a good reason of material facts, when questioned or charged, would a defendant risk an adverse inference from his silence.

Apart from the ending of the absolute right of silence, the process of assessing the credibility and reliability of material evidence remains essentially unchanged. The trial process is marginally less of a game. It has made a tentative step towards discovering the reality of a criminal event.

But it is significant that the elimination of peremptory challenges (and almost all challenges for cause) also abolished certain elements of a game, although there is some suggestion for the selectivity of the jury panel, to erase any potential prejudice. The main achievement has undoubtedly been the long lists of people who were until the 2003 Criminal Justice Act exempt from jury duty. As the press release in 2004 stated: 'Judges, politicians, vicars, bishops and lords will be able to sit on a jury ... the legislation increases significantly the number of people who can now do jury service ... around 480,000 people are summoned for jury service annually'. The jury in the twenty-first century is no longer a participant in the trial process; the court is an institution materially composed of lay persons, assisted in the process of decision-making by a judge directing the assessment of evidence and directing the amateur jurors on the relevant law.

Other than very exceptionally (when there is evidence of jury-tampering) there is no concession to any other form but jury trial. Any suggestion (of which there have been some) of a right of an accused to opt for trial by judge alone (either by choice or by waiver) is largely absent. An attempt at professional trial in serious fraud cases was tried and rejected legislatively (as described in Chapter 10). Other reforms have been directed to the form of written directions to the jury and for simplifying oral directions by the administration of questionnaires. The search for aids to reasoning decisions continues, but so long as the principle of the orality of evidence is maintained, there is not much urge to regurgitate the evidence. Despite that instruction, some judges still deliver lengthy directions – sometimes a few days – in reflecting the oral evidence of witnesses.

If, then, trial by jury gets a resounding vote of confidence, such contentment for the system lacks anything more than a profound trust in a model of tribunal that has prevailed for centuries. Yet it resides on the belief that the populace clings to its sense of popular control. The system, however, lacks any debate on its methodology of trying criminal events, the most compelling being the reasons for the verdict. At this point the jury system acknowledges the absence of a reasoned verdict. I have stressed throughout this book that the principle of a reasoned decision for any administrative act can no longer find a reasonable qualification in the process of criminal justice.

There is, however, one compelling factor that may dictate future thought. That is the cost of the trial process, not just in monetary terms but in the burden that is thrust ever more heavily on the citizen.

Participation of the lay person in the affairs of government will always persist. But lay participation finds its limitations in the quantity and quality of its use. If jury trial could be suitably circumscribed, the system would easily accommodate its users. But here there is a problem. The time devoted to the instruction may contain the seeds of its destruction, in that the citizenry seeks alternative devices for trying criminal cases. Here the evidence begins to evoke worrying factors.

At Liverpool Crown Court on 4 May 2018, a criminal trial of the owner and management of a care home in Southport for fraud offences – three conspiracies and a number of other frauds – ended, having lasted for 186 sessions over a single year. The main offender received in total 21 years of imprisonment after an egregious series of frauds upon elderly victims who yielded up their substantial incomes and savings. The trial absorbed a large amount of documentary evidence that called for careful analysis. But even this amount of evidence could have been readily handled by a professional tribunal in 3–4 months. A trial by a judge (with or without expert assessors, as was recommended by the Roskill Committee in 1984), could provide a fair trial, concluding decisively with a reasoned verdict. Such a trial which is axiomatic in civil litigation must be replicated in the criminal jurisdiction. A civil dispute, which may involve monetary consequences and other disqualifications, is certainly no less serious than the non-custodial sanctions available in the penal system.

The Liverpool experience is not unique. The growth in the power of administrative agencies such as the Finance Authority is another recent example. Disciplinary action against professionals is also widely used.

17

The Appellate Process

THE EXAGGERATED, SOMETIMES overblown, claims for the jury system, assuming positively the virtue of its inscrutable verdict, have had the direct effect of reducing the nature and scope of the appellate process. But quite apart from the absence on appeal of any review of the jury's fact-finding deliberations, the extent of the criminal justice verdict has traditionally had an inferior status to that of its civil counterpart. And however complete the summing-up by the judge to amateur jurors may be, there is no knowing whether and how much the juror has imbibed the relevant language of the judge. It was once said that even supposing the conclusions of the judge to be always plainly said and easily assimilated by each of the 12 lay jurors, it does not follow that the jury will adopt the judicial view, or, for that matter, will reject any judicial advice. To prove that the jury merely follows the summing-up would be to prove too much, since it would show that the intervention of the judge in the task of decision-making was no less superfluous than harmless. Splitting the task to arrive at a joint verdict is, in judicial terms, virtually impossible between the professional and the amateur. At best, it can strive for harmonious thought processes. At the crucial point of decision-making, the inscrutable verdict of the jury is unreviewable.

I. REFORM

The genesis of the limited appeal system is the Criminal Appeal Act 1907. The law reports of the early days of the decades before the Second World War were sparse on any legal issues in the criminal calendar. What occupied the Court of Criminal Appeal was a growing number of appeals, particularly against sentences, to which counsel for the Crown was notably not represented in the courtroom. Even when, after the War, they did appear, the convention was that their presence in the appeal was merely to assist the court, and in no sense to oppose the appeal.

That convention was largely abandoned after the change in composition of the court in 1968. But even then the assistance (badly needed, with the growing complexities of sentencing by the legislature, particularly after the Criminal Justice Act 2003, with the notorious sentences of indeterminacy in public protection cases) was often lacking. Even with the rising prison population in the twenty-first century, there is a noticeable partisanship on the part of some prosecutors. Assistance has been interpreted liberally towards ratcheting up of some sentences.

The ethos of the division of the Court of Appeal from its civil jurisdiction (with some Lords Justices declining to sit on criminal appeals) gives the unified court a distinct difference in style as well as topicality. The casual observer of criminal appeals is given the clear message that justiciability in civil and criminal cases have different connotations, not all, I would hasten to add, being uncongenial to the appealing offenders. Much about the criminality of the offender is accorded sensitive treatment; it is nevertheless dealing with a different breed of litigant. In order to demonstrate an indiscriminate attitude from the Bench, whether civil or criminal in its function, there should be no discernible difference in the rules for appealing the one from the other. Reviews of reasoned verdicts should dictate the same careful and considerate examination. If the judgment appealed against involves no reasoning, the unequal treatment would have to be transparent, at least to those desiring to know the whys and wherefores of their perceived criminality.

Once the reasoned decision is revealed, as is the evidence at trial transcripted, the appellate tribunal is equipped with all the necessary material to exercise an acceptable method of facilitating the transparency and accountability of the trial's content as well as its due process in assessing the case. One might add, argumentatively, that the relaxed reading of the printed word is to be preferred to the orality of the witnesses' statements as seen in the form of an ongoing trial. Seeing and judging the demeanour of the witness is claimed as an advantage over the unsighted appellate judge. But is that so? A witness's capacity to communicate may be conveniently concealed.

II. THE UNREASONED VERDICT ON APPEAL: UNSAFE OR UNSATISFACTORY?

If the unreasoned verdict of the jury, nevertheless, otherwise impliedly indicates its concluded view only that the verdict had been arrived at through the erroneous assessment or value of the evidence adduced in the courtroom (comprehensively directed by the trial judge), its undisclosed motive for its verdict is demonstrably unsafe. But if the jury's view resulted from an error of law, or some other irregularity has occurred in the proceedings of the criminal process, the verdict is unsatisfactory, however safe it may be to uphold the verdict. Under the Criminal Appeal Act 1968 Parliament had provided that the Court of Appeal should allow an appeal if the jury's verdict was unsafe or unsatisfactory. Under the Criminal Appeal Act 1995 the duty to acquit the accused, however, became uniform. The jury's verdict had simply to be safe, full stop. A good simile for satisfaction is statutorily a sense of fairness. Is it not possible for judges to arrive at a state of mind that concludes that the jury's verdict is unsatisfactory, but is still safe? Such a conclusion might lead to a quashing of the conviction, but might not necessarily deny the possible complicity of the appellants in the criminal event. While the presumption of innocence at trial is properly to be preserved, there is room for not concluding that the successful appeal thereby renders the accused innocent. The English statutory provision defining the criteria for a successful appeal might be deliberately dichotomous to allow for an appeal on one basis, but not on the other.

Broadly speaking (without reference to statutory construction and the jurisprudence on the criteria for allowing and dismissing appeals) the point can be put simply. If I have a spoke (or, perhaps, more than one) missing from my bicycle wheel, the vehicle is inferentially and objectively unsafe to ride. If I ride my bicycle in a wobbly fashion, my riding is unsatisfactory; it may or may not be unsafe either for myself or other road users. The test in that instance is, in part at least, subjective. But what did Parliament intend by the two words, deployed disjunctively?

The legislative origins of the two words are to be found in the debates on the Criminal Appeal Bill of 1907. FE Smith, MP for Liverpool, Walton (later to be Attorney-General and Lord Chancellor as Lord Birkenhead) moved an amendment to the Bill on 29 July 1907 directing the Court of Criminal Appeal to allow an appeal 'if they think the verdict is, under all the circumstances of the case, unsafe or unsatisfactory'. This would have replaced the formula used in respect of a jury in a civil court – namely, allow an appeal 'on any ground on which the verdict of the jury might be set aside in a civil case' – a permissible range of appeal too narrowly circumscribed. In a civil case there had to be such overwhelming preponderance of evidence as to make a verdict so unreasonable as to be perverse – that is, such a verdict as no jury, properly instructed and assisted by the judge, could return. In opposing FE Smith's amendment, but undertaking to find an acceptable alternative, the Attorney-General, Sir John Walton, said:

> The rule which would be applied if the Bill stood as drawn would be this. If the Court of Appeal thought that reasonable men properly instructed could not have arrived at the verdict at which the jury had arrived than they might set it aside, but only then. His hon. and learned friend suggested the insertion of the words 'unsafe and [*sic*] unsatisfactory'. He did not know what meaning they should attach to the words. He believed that if they were inserted it would afterwards be held that 'unsafe' must be used in connection with some canon of safety, as, for instance, danger to public safety under the conditions in which the law was being administered. The word 'unsatisfactory' was equally open to doubt, because it might be said, he thought it would be said, that an unsatisfactory verdict meant a verdict to which the existing standard of the House of Lords was applied and which showed that the verdict did not conform to that standard. He was very anxious that the matter should not be left obscure, and if his hon. and learned friend was prepared to accept the clause as it then stood he would take care that in another place the matter should be considered fully, and if words which were more satisfactory could be framed they should be framed.

Ultimately the Criminal Appeal Act 1907 empowered the court to allow an appeal on any question of law and on fact 'if they think that the verdict of the jury should be set aside on the ground that it is unreasonable or cannot be supported having regard to the evidence' – a species of unsafeness? – or 'there was a miscarriage of justice' – a species of unsatisfactoriness? Additionally an appeal could be allowed if there had been a wrong decision on any question of law. In Scotland, the English formula was adopted. The right of appeal since the Criminal Appeal (Scotland) Act 1926 includes 'any alleged miscarriage of justice in the proceedings in which he [the appellant] was convicted'. Despite the change in England, under the Criminal Appeal Act 1968, Scotland adhered to the formula of 'miscarriage of justice' in the Criminal Procedure (Scotland) Act 1975, section 228 which became the Criminal Procedure (Scotland) Act 1995, section 106, and has remained unaltered after the change in England in the Criminal Appeal Act 1995.

The FE Smith formula crept extra-statutorily into favour during the post-war years, and was specifically recommended in December 1964 by the Interdepartmental Committee on the Court of Criminal Appeal. Section 2(1)(b) of the Criminal Appeal Act 1968 provided that an appeal should be allowed if the court thinks that in either one of three situations: (a) 'the conviction [formerly 'verdict of the jury'] should be set aside on the ground that under all the circumstances of the case it is unsafe or unsatisfactory'; or (b) 'the judgment of the court of trial should be set aside on the ground of a wrong decision of any question of law'; or (c) 'there was a material irregularity in the course of the trial'.

On quashing the conviction, the Court may order a substituted verdict, or order a re-trial. The factors in deciding whether to order a re-trial are: (a) that the innocent person should be formally acquitted by a jury; (b) that a 'guilty' person should not escape justice due to a defect in the trial process.

The power to order a re-trial was little used in the immediate years after its introduction in its present form in 1968. The Runciman Commission found that its use had increased between then and the early 1990s, and recommended that more use should be made of the power. The Court was disinclined to order a re-trial whenever there had been an appreciable lapse of time between conviction and the successful appeal.

If the Court of Appeal does not order a substituted verdict or a re-trial, the quashing of the conviction operates as a direction to the chief clerk of the Crown Court to enter an acquittal. That piece of administrative machinery merely perfects the order of wrongful conviction. As Dr Pattenden rightly comments: 'Acquittal by direction of the Court of Appeal should not be regarded as a finding of innocence'.

There is no question of any revival of the presumption of innocence, which persists only so long as the jury does not record a verdict of guilty. Once that happens, the contrary is proved; the presumption is displaced ('rebutted' in the lawyer's language). The reasons are plain. First, there is nothing in the legislation which authorises the Court of Appeal, in quashing a conviction, to say whether it thinks that the successful appellant is innocent. One reason is that in our criminal justice system it is not just those who are actually innocent who are entitled to have their convictions quashed. Those, for example, who have been prejudiced by a want of due process (not having had a fair trial) are entitled to the same result. Sir Frederick Lawton, a distinguished Lord Justice of Appeal from 1972 to 1986 – he had been a High Court judge experienced in criminal trials since 1961 – has been quoted as having once remarked how 'extremely irritating' it is to see a person who has had his conviction quashed 'prancing in front of the television cameras saying: "I have been proven innocent"'.

There is another reason, advanced by the purists among the legal profession. It is claimed that the jury has not even the power to declare someone innocent. Despite a common popular view to the contrary, a verdict of not guilty does not mean that the accused was not responsible for the crime; it means only that in law he must be treated as if he did not commit it. As Professor Zander, a member of the Runciman Commission, put it in an article in *The Times* in 1994:

> It is true that as a principle of our system there is a presumption of innocence. But that does not mean that an acquittal officially serves as a declaration of innocence. The presumption of innocence exists quite independently of whether the defendant is innocent or guilty, and indeed has nothing to do with the question of guilt or otherwise.

'Not guilty' may often arouse the feeling of 'not proved', but the intermediate verdict of 'not proven' in Scottish criminal procedure has no counterpart in England. The effect of a 'not proven' verdict is the same as that of 'not guilty', in that the accused is released and cannot be tried again for that offence. The implication, however, is that he has escaped conviction only because of some slight (not wholly unreasonable) doubt or some technicality in the trial process. It is claimed by Scottish lawyers that the 'not proven' verdict is a valuable preventive against unjustified verdicts of not guilty, but it is rarely used in Scottish trials.

III. THE ORIGINS OF THE GROUNDS FOR ALLOWING CRIMINAL APPEALS

Before questioning the Court of Appeal's conclusions on the proper construction of section 2(1)(b) of the 1968 Act, it is necessary to complete the legislative history.

The three grounds for allowing an appeal – a wrong decision on any question of law, a material irregularity in the course of the trial, and a conviction which is unsafe or unsatisfactory – are replaced in the Criminal Appeal Act 1995 by a single ground that the Court of Appeal 'think that the conviction is unsafe'. This dropping of the disjunctive phrase, in favour of the single ground, followed the recommendations of the Runciman Commission on Criminal Procedure in 1991. The change in England did not find favour in Scotland. A report of the Independent Committee on Criminal Appeals and Miscarriages of Justice Procedures (the Sutherland Committee) to the Secretary of State for Scotland in June 1996 adhered to the 'miscarriage of justice' formula. It said:

> We do not believe that the case has been made by the proponents of change for abandoning the concept of 'miscarriage of justice' as the ground for an appeal. Nor do we believe that, if change were to be necessary, it would be acceptable to move to the formulation of a conviction being 'unsafe'. There is no body of Scottish jurisprudence which relates to the concept of

an 'unsafe' verdict. It would be a novel concept in Scottish criminal law. By contrast the ground of 'miscarriage of justice' and the scope of the Appeal Court's powers in relation to the disposal of appeals have been in use for a considerable period of time and have been judicially considered and clarified in many cases in a way which shows them to be capable of adaptation and development to meet contemporary understandings of justice in criminal appeals. This approach is firmly rooted in the Scottish legal system and offers suitable flexibility. We regard this as the best and most appropriate way forward in Scottish circumstances.

The genesis of the phrase 'unsafe or unsatisfactory' pre-dated its introduction in 1966. Apart from FE Smith's attempt in 1907 to persuade Parliament to anticipate the legislative provision of 60 years later, the Court of Criminal Appeal between 1907 and the late 1960s had used such extra-statutory language in performance of the statutory duty to allow or dismiss an appeal. An indication of that judicial approach was elucidated in 1994 in the High Court of Australia in *M v The Queen*.[1] The test for applying section 6(1) of the Criminal Appeal Act 1912 (New South Wales) – a replicate of section 4(1) of the English Criminal Appeal Act 1907 – is as follows: namely, the Court will allow an appeal if:

> of opinion that the verdict of the jury can be set aside on the ground that it is unreasonable, or cannot be supported, having regard to the evidence, or that the judgment of the court of trial should be set aside on the ground of a wrong decision on any question of law, or that on any other ground whatsoever there was a miscarriage of justice.

The majority of the High Court of Australia said:

> Where a court of criminal appeal sets aside a verdict on the ground that it is unreasonable or cannot be supported having regard to the evidence, it frequently does so expressing its conclusion in terms of a verdict which is unsafe or unsatisfactory. Other terms may be used such as 'unjust or unsafe' or 'dangerous or unsafe'. In reaching such a conclusion, the court does not consider as a question of law whether there is evidence to support the verdict. Questions of law are separately dealt with by s 6(1). The question is one of fact which the court must decide by making its own independent assessment of the evidence and determining whether, notwithstanding that there is evidence upon which a jury might convict 'nonetheless it would be dangerous in all the circumstances to allow the verdict of guilty to stand'. But a verdict may be unsafe or unsatisfactory for reasons which lie outside the formula requiring that it be not 'unreasonable' or incapable of being 'supported

---

[1] *M v The Queen* [1994] HCA 63, 181 CLR 487.

having regard to the evidence'. A verdict which is unsafe or unsatisfactory for any other reason must also constitute a miscarriage of justice requiring the verdict to be set aside. In speaking of the Criminal Appeal Act in *Hargan v R*, Mr Justice Isaacs said:

> If [the appellant] can show a miscarriage of justice, that is sufficient. That is the greatest innovation made by the Act, and to lose sight of that is to miss the point of the legislative advance.

The High Court also said:

> The test [for allowing an appeal] ... is the discernment of a verdict that is unsafe or unsatisfactory. That does not call for the application of what has been called a 'speculative or intuitive basis' and does not extend to the English subjective test that an Appeal Court discern 'some lurking doubt in our minds which makes us wonder whether an injustice has been done'. The question, in Australia, is one of fact which the court decides, making its own independent assessment of the evidence: in so doing it assesses whether, on the whole of the evidence, it was open to the jury to be satisfied beyond reasonable doubt that the accused was guilty. The court will not allow itself to substitute trial by court of appeal for trial by jury, for the ultimate question must always go back to determining whether the jury could have been satisfied beyond reasonable doubt.

The pinpointing of 'miscarriage of justice', favoured by the Scots lawyers, has never found universal favour in English judicial circles; hence its partial abandonment in 1966 and its final demise in 1995, with the removal of its negative form in the proviso to the grounds for allowing an appeal. The essence of the problem lies in the extent to which Parliament in 1968 was merely giving declaratory effect to the judicial language, or was deliberately giving differential effect to the two disjunctive words.

IV. A QUESTION OF STATUTORY CONSTRUCTION

As Lord Reid said in *R v Federal Steam Navigation Co Ltd*,[2] it would be quite wrong for any court to construe a disjunctive phrase, such as safe *and* satisfactory, conjunctively. Lord Reid went on to say that, nevertheless, there was another applicable principle of construction:

> In very limited classes of circumstances, it has been held proper to strike out a word from a statute or other writing and to substitute one or more other words for the words struck out.

---

[2] *R v Federal Steam Navigation Co Ltd* [1973] 3 All ER 849, CA.

But there is no authority that I am aware of that displaces the primary task of giving every word used by the legislature some meaning. The Court may not simply pronounce that Parliament has indulged in a piece of supererogation by the use of two words meaning precisely the same, unless the words are manifestly interchangeable. 'Unsafe' is not linguistically the same as 'unsatisfactory'. Quite the contrary.

In the *Federal Steam Navigation* case, Lord Wilberforce began his judgment thus:

> My Lords, it is important to state precisely what we are asked to decide in this appeal. It is to determine the meaning of the following phrase – extracted from section 1(1) of the Oil in Navigable Waters Act 1955:
>
>> If any oil ... is discharged from a British Ship ... the owner or master of the ship shall, ... be guilty of an offence under this section.
>
> To say that what we have to decide is whether 'or' is conjunctive or disjunctive, or, putting it more bluntly, whether 'or' means 'and', appears to me, with respect, to be a dangerous simplification. It is the meaning of the phrase as a whole that concerns us.

All the Law Lords in that case agreed that the courts had power to treat the section as though the relevant words were 'the owner and/or the master'. What divided the House was the question whether the concept of a criminal offence gave the Crown an unfettered discretion to select which of the two persons should be criminally liable. The result was to avoid such a legal monstrosity by applying 'surgery rather than therapeutics'. In logic, there was no rule that required that 'or' should carry an exclusive force.

By parity of reason it would be a legal monstrosity to suggest that both concepts 'unsafe' and 'unsatisfactory' had to be satisfied before a conviction could be set aside or, as a matter of language, that they should be treated tautologously. Adopting Lord Wilberforce's approach, what is the meaning of the phrase in section 2(1) of the Criminal Appeal Act 1968 as a whole? The phrase is '... the Court of Appeal shall allow an appeal against conviction if they think – (a) that the conviction should be set aside on the ground that under all the circumstances of the case it is unsafe or unsatisfactory'.

The first thing to note is that the statute is dealing exclusively with the appellate function of the criminal law; it does not disturb the 'diacritical variant' – the mark of distinguishing the different values of acquittal and conviction – of the trial verdict. Quite the contrary, it does not extinguish or nullify the verdict of guilt; it only sets it aside. The *New Shorter Oxford English Dictionary* (1993) gives as the primary meaning of 'set aside', 'discontinue the performance or practice of' or 'dismiss from consideration' and only secondarily, 'reject as of no value, cogency or pertinence; overrule; discard or reject from use or service, in favour of another'. An alternative meaning given is '(chiefly Law) annul, quash, make void, vacate'.

If section 2(1)(a) was to be read as a whole, may it not have been Parliament's intention (as evinced by the true meaning of what they said) to confer a power on the Court of Appeal to allow an appeal if it thought that the conviction should no longer have any practical effect for either one or other of two alternative reasons? Thus it would be left to the appeal court to distinguish between the unsound verdict of guilt based on the material adduced before the jury (and any other additional evidence) and the conviction which was arrived at by a failure in the application of due process without detracting from the content and substance of the evidential material.

V. UNSAFE OR UNSATISFACTORY: WHICH?

The proposal of the Royal Commission on Criminal Justice (the Runciman Commission) in 1993 was to replace the existing law with a general broad ground – whether the conviction 'is or may be unsafe'. The effect of that proposal was that convictions would in the future not be quashed where, despite an error of law or a material irregularity in the trial process or pre-trial malpractice by the police or prosecution, the conviction remained 'safe'. The Home Office in its discussion paper on the Runciman proposal endorsed the view that the Court of Appeal should be concerned only with the safety of the conviction and not with acting as a 'quasi-disciplinary body, "punishing" errors or incompetence in the trial process'. Safety (unqualified by a 'may be') of conviction became the sole criterion in the 1995 Act for allowing an appeal.

If there had to be a choice between the supposedly interchangeable words, 'unsatisfactory' rather than 'unsafe' would seem to be preferred, so as to reflect the Runciman Commission's otherwise expressed desire to encourage a greater willingness in the appellate system to interfere with jury verdicts. 'Unsatisfactory' is a good word, since it covers anything ranging from 'there is something fishy', alternatively, 'a lurking doubt' about this conviction, to a closely reasoned demolition job by defence counsel of the evidential material. If in effect one were to draw a circle containing all the things that are unsatisfactory in the arrival of a guilty verdict, 'unsafe' would certainly be inside this circle. 'Safe', or any equivalent words, would, however, have to be encompassed by a separate circle. The difficulty about the all-encompassing use of 'unsatisfactory' is that it would sound odd for prosecuting counsel to describe the jury's verdict as satisfactory, when the attack by the defence is directed to an evaluation of the evidence – 'my Lords, the evidence was in a satisfactory state for the jury to convict'. 'Unsatisfactory' is appropriate, however, when limited to a material irregularity in the trial process, which does not affect the quality of the evidence.

Did Parliament in the Criminal Appeal Act 1995, in its perceived resolution of the debate, in fact deliberately abandon the dichotomy between 'unsafe' and 'unsatisfactory', and did it not simply endorse the ruling of the Court of Appeal that the words were interchangeable, and hence prefer to use one word instead of two? After all, as I have indicated, an unsafe verdict is by definition unsatisfactory, but not vice versa. What do we mean by safe – safe from what? Safe from a humiliating appeal decision? Safe, as it were, from the indignation and reproaches of the person convicted, or from the criticism of academic lawyers, or of society in general? Or do we express the sense of a verdict being *secure* or impregnable against any critical analysis (forensic, in all senses, or academic or armchair, logical or factual, or whatever)? We could do some thesaurus-thumbing, looking for words which we might use informally, like *unassailable, watertight, certain, well-founded, solid, reliable, conclusive*, or perhaps best of all, *incontrovertible*.

An appellate court may properly say the conviction (or the verdict of the jury) is 'unsafe', in that it is clear that the convicted person, who was found guilty on the evidence adduced at trial, should not have been convicted. Apart from the tricky cases where fresh evidence is admitted by the Court of Appeal and the court has to evaluate the totality of evidence (the evidence at trial, plus the fresh evidence) the 'safe' conviction or verdict may nevertheless be 'unsatisfactory', in the sense that there has been some procedural irregularity which renders the trial 'unfair'. The words 'unsafe' and 'unsatisfactory' are not linguistically interchangeable, although both are ultimately Latin derivatives. The reason why English lawyers have tended to treat the words tautologously is the diacritical variant of English law – the black and white of guilt or innocence. As Lord Gifford QC neatly said: 'English law does not recognise two categories of acquittal; nor should it recognise two categories of successful appeal'. We do not, however, need to emulate Scots law, and confuse the trial jury with an alternative verdict of 'not proven'. Innocence until proven guilty is a healthy maxim for a civilised society to adopt up to the moment of primarily establishing criminal responsibility at trial. To maintain innocence beyond the point of failure to sustain a conviction on appeal, which relates to some irregularity, is not an imperative. Irregularity in the trial process does not displace the integrity of proven complicity as a result of the jury's verdict on the evidence, particularly where the evidence was circumstantial and had not been displaced.

Three members of the Runciman Commission, in dissenting from the majority of their colleagues, thought that it would be confusing to wrap up all the possible grounds of appeal in the one word 'unsafe'. They considered:

> ... that the grounds of appeal should be redrafted to take into account two separate categories of appeal, those claiming that the verdict had been arrived at through an erroneous view of the evidence by the jury ... and those alleging material irregularities or errors of law or procedures in or before the trial.

This sound reasoning went unheeded.

There was some discussion during the committee stage of the Criminal Appeal Bill 1995 of the exact meaning of the word 'unsafe'. The Home Office minister, Mr Nicholas Baker, stated that the compendious term was intended to consolidate the existing practice of the Court of Appeal, thus rejecting the notion that 'unsafe' and 'unsatisfactory' are different concepts. He preferred to take up another test that may be found in decisions of the Court of Appeal, namely, that a 'lurking doubt' exists as to whether the conviction may stand. While this may simply be another way of expressing the word 'unsafe', it does not appear in the previous or present legislation. Whenever a court puts a gloss on statutory criteria there is a danger of moving away from those words towards some other formula not intended by Parliament to be used.

In practice the Court of Appeal pre-1995 rarely invited argument as to the precise meaning of the two words; nor did it pay much attention to the structure of its statutory jurisdiction. In 1968 in *R v Cooper*[3] Lord Widgery, commenting on section 4 of the Criminal Appeal Act 1966, said that the judges had to form a subjective opinion on whether they had a 'lurking doubt' about the correctness of the verdict. He added that 'this is a reaction which may not be based strictly on the evidence as such; it is a reaction which can be produced by the general feel of the case as the court experiences it'. This was the first occasion on which the Court had the opportunity of commenting on the new formula of 'unsafe or

---

[3] *R v Cooper* [1969] 1 QB 267.

unsatisfactory'. However, in *R v Wellington*[4] Lord Lane rejected this test as too subjective and spoke of the need for a 'reasoned and substantial unease' about the conviction in juxtaposition to assessing whether the conviction was 'safe *and* satisfactory' (italics supplied).

The only reported case I have been able to find where a very definite distinction was drawn between 'unsafe' and 'unsatisfactory' is *R v Llewellyn*.[5] Lord Justice (later Lord) Roskill said, in that case, where the appeal was founded on an improper indication from the trial judge of the consequences of plea bargaining, that the decision would be quashed for unfairness '*not that it is unsafe but that it is unsatisfactory*'. He emphasised that the appellant was very fortunate, given the evidence and the fair conduct of the remainder of the trial and the lack of any mitigation in the circumstances of the offence.

The Antipodean approach in *M v The Queen* fulfils the function of the evaluation of evidential material so as to determine criminal responsibility. It does not touch on those matters that are not within the jury's function and go to due process which may render the trial unfair (or unsatisfactory). As Sir John Smith QC argued in an article in the *New Law Journal* in 1995, an example of the procedural irregularity was demonstrable in the case of *R v Algar*[6] – a pre-1968 Act case. The conviction in that case was quashed because the appellant's wife, who was an incompetent witness, had been improperly allowed to give evidence at the trial. The Lord Chief Justice, Lord Goddard, told the appellant that he had a lucky escape: 'Do not think we are doing this because we think that you are an innocent man. We do not. We think you are a scoundrel' – an unsatisfactory verdict, but certainly not unsafe. Now that under the 1995 Act the Court of Appeal has lost its power to apply the proviso ['notwithstanding the court might decide in favour of the appellant, it can dismiss the appeal if it considers that no miscarriage of justice has actually occurred'] it may have to confirm a conviction, however unsatisfactory the trial has been, so long as the procedural irregularity has not endangered the safety of the conviction. Mr Baker thought that the word 'unsafe' would cover procedural irregularities such as to make the verdict unacceptable. That is unsatisfactory – linguistically, at least.

However, during the passage of the Bill through both Houses of Parliament, there was no questioning of the conclusive view of the Court

---

[4] *R v Wellington* [1991] Crim LR 543, CA.
[5] *R v Llewellyn* (1978) 67 Cr App Rep 149.
[6] *R v Algar* [1954] 1 QB 279.

of Appeal that the words 'unsafe' and 'unsatisfactory' were interchangeable. Indeed, one MP, Mr (now Sir) Oliver Heald, a practising barrister until he became a junior minister in 1995, went so far as to say that he knew nobody who could tell him the difference between an 'unsafe' and an 'unsatisfactory' conviction. Only Lord McIntosh of Haringey, a non-lawyer, speaking for the Labour opposition, said that he did not agree that the words bore no difference in meaning but had to concede that 'for practical purposes, we agree that there is no distinction'. The only debate on the proposed grounds for allowing an appeal was a minor departure from the recommendations of the Runciman Commission which had opted for the formula 'unsafe or may be unsafe'. In moving the second reading of the Bill, the Home Secretary said:

> The Bill clarifies the grounds for allowing appeals on three overlapping grounds which is widely felt to cause confusion. Under the Bill, the Court of Appeal will allow any appeal where it considers the conviction to be unsafe and will dismiss it in any other case. This simple test clarifies the terms of the existing practice of the Court of Appeal, and I am pleased to note that the Lord Chief Justice has already welcomed it.

When the Bill went to the House of Lords, Lord Taylor, the Lord Chief Justice, did indeed support the Government's suggested change in the language for setting aside a jury's verdict, and added for good measure that there was no merit in including in the simple test the words 'or may be unsafe'. He considered that the implication of doubt was inherent in the single word 'unsafe'.

It is puzzling to note that nowhere was any mention made, if only of rejection, of the dissenting note of the three members of the Runciman Commission, including the relevant passage in Professor Zander's personal note of dissent.

According to DW Broeder,[7] two factors are claimed to induce trust in trial by jury. The first is that the 'community is said to have more confidence in the judgment of laymen than of those learned in the law'. The second is that 'complex and sometimes insoluble factual disputes have the appearance of being settled with ease when wrapped in the silent garb of a verdict returned in supposed compliance with strict legal rules'. But, as Norval Morris points out, we know almost nothing of what thought processes go on in the jury room. At present we are denied by statute the possibility of learning about or researching into juries.

---

[7] See his article 'The Functions of the Jury' (1954) 21 *Chicago Law Review* 386, 417.

Criminal justice has the laudable aim to infuse the system with all the safeguards of due process. Linguistically, the words 'unsafe or unsatisfactory' have different meanings, to which the courts should have given legal effect. The strength of evidential material and the process by which it is adduced are two methods whereby the courts can effect the quality of judicial service.

Lord Devlin once wrote that 'the sleep of the final verdict is disturbed by the nightmare of miscarriage'. So it should be, but we should not allow the verdict of the jury – the sole determiners of fact – to be awakened from its peaceful slumbers by anything that is simply called by the name of miscarriage of justice (or a carriage of misjustice, as one commentator observed). Nightmares should be sparingly experienced, only when the moral conscience is properly aroused. Perhaps the discombobulation which is felt about some of the verdicts of our criminal courts – perverse acquittals as well as wrongful convictions – can be appropriately allayed and suitably corrected on appeal, only as and when decision-makers are called upon to articulate fully the reasons for their decisions.

Insistence on reasoned verdicts would lead to the demise, or rejection, by choice, of trial by jury. No 12 good men or women could compose proper, adequate and intelligent reasons this side of Doomsday. It is a daunting thought, not to be contemplated by the proponents of trial by jury, let alone by a civilised society. But so long as we cling to the fundamental right to jury trial for all serious offences, and endow the jury with the exclusive power to determine guilt or not, we must not be too assiduous in calling its verdicts into question. The danger is that, if no restraint is exercised, we will seriously undermine public confidence in the criminal justice system.

The Interdepartmental Committee on Jury Service in 1965 stated that it was vitally important that the system of trial by jury should be 'fair, sensible and workable' for 'ensuring law and order are maintained, that justice is done and that liberties are to be preserved'. It concluded, however, that it did not wish to prejudice any future inquiry into the merits of the jury system, 'as to which we realise that there is room for divergent views'. Has the time come for that 'future inquiry' and for airing 'the divergent views'?

Dicey wrote in his *Law of the Constitution*:[8]

> A distinguished French thinker [unidentified] may be right in holding that the habit of submitting difficult problems of fact to the decision of twelve men

[8] 9th edn (1945) 394.

of not more than average education and intelligence, will in the near future be considered an absurdity as patent as ordeal by battle.

Dicey added his own view that trial by jury was sustainable only so long as public confidence (or perhaps blind faith) resided in the system. If the view of the French 'thinker' is somewhat extreme, the idea that the guilt or innocence of an accused person can be appropriately determined by the say-so of 12 ordinary citizens, without giving any reasons for their verdict (and no accountability for a perverse acquittal) may soon come to be regarded as either unsafe or unsatisfactory, such as to undermine public confidence that we operate in Britain a civilised system of criminal justice. Furthermore, it is no longer true that a plaintiff in a libel action has a right to insist on trial by a jury.

One might echo the words of Professor Jose Correa, the former Chief of Staff of the Chilean National Commission on Truth and Reconciliation:

Although the truth cannot really dispense justice, it does put an end to many a continued injustice. It does not bring the dead back to life but it brings them out from silence.

Conclusion

THE EXCURSUS OF this book has thrown up two contemporary curiosities. First, the compelling attraction by the populace of trial by one's peers is loud and voluble. Such popularity is culturally presumed, even if it can safely be said that it is on the wane, prompted nowadays by the inherent feature that the jurors are infected by the modern world of social media and information technology, increasingly at play in criminal trials. Science and technology often render the exercise of decision-making by lay participants in lengthier and complicated trials much more problematic, in the sense that the evidential material may often be unfamiliar to the layman. Elucidation of such evidence by the advocates and the trial judge in his summing up and direction of the jury is regarded as a serious factor in the juror's understanding of the evidence. Some of the unfamiliar evidence can have its esoteric mystery dispelled; to many jurors, reliance is placed on the forensic process, which may nevertheless instil bewilderment or bemusement. Judges in their summings-up undoubtedly seek to assist the jury in its understanding of the evidence, but we can never know precisely the scope and nature of the understanding (or misunderstanding) arising from the alchemy of judge and juror(s). There are some research studies that reveal the extent of jurors not understanding – at least not fully understanding – the evidence, and even disapplying the law as iterated by the trial judge.

The dichotomy (or, if you prefer, the unspoken dialogue) of the two separate functions – director and directed – is complicated by the distinct absence from a jury verdict of any reasoned verdict. As Lord Brown (a distinguished Law Lord in both the judicial House of Lords and its successor, the UK Supreme Court) in his Oxford lecture in 2010 noted, the absence of reasons is the clinching fact in wanting to reform the system. The merits of any socially important decision-maker depend quintessentially on the practice of ratiocination, the process of the articulation of thought in the procedure of formulation and conclusion of the reasoning. In the most compelling conduct of the state by way of intervention in the citizen's civil liberty – the most exacting form of interference – it is relied upon. It is not just a fine thought of the legal scholar. It pervades social consciousness.

The second curiosity is that the popular attitude varies according to the nature of the criminality under investigation. It is no surprise that the vagaries of fraudulent conduct have been singled out for specialist treatment. There is a marked attempt by many parliamentarians to convert trial of serious fraudsters to a professional tribunal, either judge alone or a judge sitting with professionals from the world of economics and finance.

This digression on the models of tribunal for serious crime demonstrates that a uniform mode of trial will not fit all circumstances of criminal justice. Forensic evidence in homicide cases often calls for expert medical evidence that might suggest trial by professionals. Already in recent years, emergency situations arising out of terrorism are now a common feature. When there is strong evidence of tampering with the jury, specialist trials may be indicated. Types of criminal offence may indicate specialist trials. But which? There will undoubtedly be need for a body that initially manages the form of trial. I call it the Management Committee for Criminal Justice. At the core of the distribution of the mode of trial, there is still the need for choice – the right of an accused to opt for trial by jury.

This chapter spells out the main grounds for a new system of dualistic modes of trial for serious crime. The variety of systems must now replace the system of trial by jury. Jury trial was a socially acceptable system, so long as the jurors came democratically from a largely illiterate society. But that pre-Enlightenment feature of the common law has had its time – except for those who choose not to know why they are found guilty or innocent. As Jeremy Bentham said in 1790, jury trial is barbaric to the world of the Enlightenment.

If there is a general consensus in civilised societies that every person charged with a criminal offence of a serious nature is entitled to a fair trial before an independent and impartial tribunal in open justice, there is a growing discord about a uniform mode of trial. The jury is out, on that issue. The decision to find guilt or innocence, either by the single composition of jurors, or in part by lay participation in a judicial institution, is currently under threat, mainly because of the increasing complexities of criminal offences and the time taken for trial. Added to that, the clamour for both greater transparency and public accountability has contributed to the virtues of today's criminal jurisdiction.

Fact-finding of the events concerning a criminal act calls for an ability of common experience, subject of course to personal disposition to what we all see, or hear. The forensic process of deliberation and recording the judgment of criminality requires altogether a different skill and talent.

The process calls for a professionalism that is absent from the amateur. The supply of reasons for the tribunal's conclusion of guilt or innocence is altogether a task of justiciability (an ugly but effective word). The unreasoned (or imperfectly reasoned) verdict is highly questionable. The reason is clear. Historically, the forensic process was all of a piece. While the prospective jury was from an illiterate, if undemocratic, community, an unqualified verdict was entirely acceptable. Our masters, all property owners until 1972, knew what was good for us all. Now, enhanced by information technology, we insist that whatever we undergo should be explained in language that is intelligible. From the contemporary requirement that the trial judge should sum up the relevant facts for the jury to understand the issues, it follows that the defendant should be able to know the reasons for the verdict. As the European Court at Strasbourg indicated, it is necessary for the defendant to understand fully the reasons for the verdict, otherwise there cannot be a fair trial. Fairness is not just procedural; it is in substance fairly grounded. Fairness demands articulation of a fair verdict.

The focus on the verdict, as distinguished from the process to arrive at it, is a separate right that the law should grant to the defendant as a distinct aspect of a fair trial. Society's attitude to the split process calls for separate treatment, and an adequate response from the decision-maker at trial. Being told why the process is concluded against (or for) the defendant is a human right. What then, should the mode of trial be for its pronounced verdict? It is because of this dual function that a recognition of the subject should be considered.

If the criminal offence involves some domestic violence or even any offence against the person, the nature of the trial is likely to focus on issues of common experience, understandable by the reasonable juror. It may also mean that the consequence of physical violence on the victim can readily be judged. The fact-finding and the decision-making are easily determinable, both in fact and in law. If, however, the criminal offence is a property offence, or an aspect of fraudulent conduct, the knowledge may be quite different. The scope of fraudulent conduct is frequently so wide as to be beyond the purview of the ordinary citizen. Understanding complicated facts demands specialist knowledge of the corporate or complicated fraud. It is at this point that the defendant should be allowed to express his defence to those who will understand the nature of the conduct. It is not irrelevant, moreover, that the length of fraud trials imposes a heavy duty on the juror or lay participant in the process. At the extreme end of the scale, as noted in Chapter 16, is the recent case (ending on 4 May 2018) in Liverpool Crown Court which ran to 186 days over a whole year of trial. These factors explain the various attempts by authorities to replace the jury with a professionally-composed court, made up of judges plus those with expertise in financial affairs – until now unsuccessful. The time is ripe, therefore, for reform. The approach should mean that in the case of particular offences, the mode of trial should be by professionals only, or by judge and appointed experts. Emergency cases, such as political offences and terrorist crimes, require specialist (professional) treatment. To administer a system where there must be a selection of the appropriate mode of trial calls for the establishment in criminal justice administration of an official body to order the appropriate criminal court. A Criminal Cases Management Committee should be established to determine the type of court appropriate for the trial. At that preliminary hearing the defendant should be able to choose the court. Trial by jury (as now) should be available, as well as alternative models.

No one should interpret the authorship of this book as a case for the abolition of the jury system (English style) as a model of a fair trial of serious offences in the criminal jurisdiction. Far from it: the question of any reform of trial by jury is essentially political, even depending on other than its assumed, constitutional status. Inherent trust in the reasonably intelligent man or woman, or the professionally qualified arbiter, is at the heart of the choice. The reasons for recording a verdict of guilt (or innocence) are likewise essential to a fair trial. The jury is embedded in the Anglo-Saxon mind. Belief, Bertrand Russell once observed, dies hard, and only when presented with irrefutable evidence and political change should we dispense with our juridical culture. But reform is ripe to effect a criminal justice system fit for the twenty-first century. The attributes of a fair trial, imposed municipally in October 2000 by the Human Rights Act 1998, were bound to influence the established system.

No one single mode of trial seems to fit the bill of trial for serious criminal offences. All of them have their supporters and detractors, although there is a preponderance of the amalgam of the professional judge and the skilled layman working together in assessing the credibility of testimony and the reliability of witnesses in the process of decision-making. Somehow, the two components work together elsewhere in modern society. In general, professionals and lay decision-makers support working in unison as a panel in differing proportions. The inherent problem envisaged by commentators is the supposed dominance of professional judges either as the judge and jury that take place in whole trials, as the sign of criminal justice as a whole in the form of a judge or a panel with lay judges. Philosophically, citizen participation is construed as one of the most important aspects of democracy in the courts, which is politically desirable. Other critics support the Dutch system (as I do), believing that no form of lay adjudication should ever be possible in the legal system. Trial by a professional judiciary is a minimum requirement. There is no place for the amateur in our system of criminal justice, just as there is no place for punishment in our penal system, as Isaiah Berlin observed in his inaugural lecture on Two Concepts of Liberty at Oxford in 1957.

One senses that the search for one uniform model of court in Europe is unattainable, or at least unattainable with anything approaching public acceptance. Indeed, any unison of thought seems to broaden out in arguments for reform. There is a countervailing sense that different forms of criminality call for different modes of trial, the one common factor being the explanation for the verdict. Even where the decision-maker is not debarred from a reasoned judgment, the product is either insufficiently articulated or the reasoning itself does not satisfy the appetite of the parties involved or the wider public.

This author concludes that one mode of criminal trial cannot fit all criminal offences; each class of crime dictates the approach of those concluding the nature and scope of the crime adduced evidentially. Hence, the criminal justice system must adapt its mode of trial according to established criteria, including importantly a general right in the accused to seek trial by jury; in so doing, that defendant forgoes the human right to be given the reasons for the jury verdict.

This book is an overall analysis of society's choice for establishing a fair trial. The merits and demerits of the system are exposed for evaluation of the style of jury trial which demands by specific oath a monosyllabic verdict, reasoned only indirectly by a judicial summing-up, the judge's duty to direct and guide, so that the offender and the wider public are sufficiently satisfied of a fair trial. Given the function of jury trial in its present form, it must be assumed that there is general acceptability for trial by a non-professional tribunal. But, taking into full consideration the nascent call for greater transparency and accountability in public administration, the need for a rational choice of a populist system is evident, but it should be available only at the defendant's insistence.

One needs to acknowledge that the jury system is a publicly acceptable solution in the criminal jurisdiction on the grounds of our unique culture that is often infused with innate prejudice. Preconception and prejudice, neither of which is to be confused with bias (which is altogether another dimension of human perception of government), which we all possess from birth onwards, in one form or another. It is the role of the decider (the jury or other model) to recognise any indirect prejudice, and then seek to put it aside in the process of deliberation. That differentiation between the professional (the judge) and the amateur (layman, drawn from the electorate) is at the heart of the basic choice. A judgment which is well reasoned is intrinsically a judicial feature of a fair trial. Its absence is crucial, but not exclusive.

Choice of mode of trial was made politically in 1934 when all civil trials (with the limited exception of libel actions) were rendered jury-less. Why should the determination of criminal liability not go down the same route? That is the question to which this book seeks to supply the rational answer in a modern society. Historically, the two jurisdictions developed separately, but that may not be enough to satisfy the symmetry of the legal system. Are their ingredients quite different in kind? Do they warrant separate treatment in human rights? In one sense, that already happens. Every day the law courts are occupied by judges in the Chancery Division trying insolvency and fraud cases that are evidentially indistinguishable from the criminal fraud cases being heard down the road at Old Bailey. All fraudulent behaviour calls for the same judicial treatment.

If a fair trial is the essence of both the civil and criminal jurisdictions, is there any reason to vary the concept of fairness between the two? Surely not. Fairness is a relative, not an absolute concept, directed at the verdict, not just at the due process. It is fairness with respect to particular conditions or results. The law takes meticulous care that a person charged with a crime, whatever form the investigation and trial procedure takes, is given the opportunity to defend himself. Whatever be the pressure of incriminating proof, the high standard of proof is inviolate and exists irrespective of the decision-maker's standard of proof. The only acceptable limitation is that fairness is due to both the accused and the accuser. Although I eschew references to the jury system in the USA, I cannot restrain from citing the words of Justice Benjamin Cardozo in *Syndner v Massachusetts*,[1] that 'the concept of fairness must not be strained till it is narrowed to a filament. We are to keep the balance true'. Even-handedness is the counterpart concept.

Fairness can be primarily enhanced by two reforms. First, the complexities of fraudulent conduct argue favourably, as did the Roskill Committee in 1986, for a professional tribunal. The other reform

---

[1] *Syndner v Massachusetts* 291 US 97 (1934) at 105–106.

introduces a system of waiver, the choice between the professional and the amateur. Choice is not new; in 1790 Jeremy Bentham said that jury trial was absurdly defective; the offender should be allowed to choose it if he wished. But are there any other types of criminality that should be separately tried? The two that come to mind are homicide offences and cases of domestic violence. Both these kinds of criminal behaviour need professional judgment, together with forensic expertise provided in the form of testimony to the judge on law. Domestic violence may also need the particular skills of a family law judge and social service workers. For 35 years (1972–2007) Diplock Courts delivered justice in Northern Ireland. The experience of juryless trials is not unknown to British justice, even if the devotion to trial by one's fellow citizens still rules the roost. Jury trial should survive, but only if justice demands that the choice is reasonable.

Nowadays there is serious discussion about the topic of alternative dispute resolution. This ongoing debate about the alternatives to litigation stems from an overwhelming desire prompted by inordinate delay and excessive cost in the established legal system. Access to justice is no longer about the availability of litigation in the courts of law; cheaper ways of resolving disputes between citizens, and more particularly of complaints against public administration, are being sought. Whatever be the high quality of the judicial decision-making in the High Court and the Crown Courts in this country, the recent years of escalating costs in public funding – and in particular, the widespread loss of legal aid from public sources – have accelerated the process. Disputants against public administration are invited, almost deliberately, to choose to resolve disputes outside of the courts of law. For the commercial world there has always been the traditional route of arbitration, primarily motivated by a process which, although controlled in law by the court system, could be conducted privately between disputants, in secret. But arbitration is itself a costly exercise, although it maintains other advantages to the commercial litigant.

Arbitration apart, and given the judicial use of litigation to settle or resolve publicly their dispute, the citizen has, since the end of the Second World War, had recourse to methods of conciliation by other devices when faced with disagreement with public administration. The advent of the Ombudsman (known officially as the Parliamentary Commissioner for Administration) in 1967 allowed people to seek a suitable resolution of any administrative dispute from the administration, via the Ombudsman. Their complaint had to be channelled through the relevant Member of Parliament. But it was soon extended to local

government, where no such formal application had to be politically regis-
tered. Ombudsmanry was speedily adopted by a number of organisations
administering problems that came within their province, including trade
associations that organised themselves as a private institution.

All of these developments implicitly depended on the citizen's
exercise of a right to reasons for some, otherwise unresolved, issues.
Choice of access to justice was ever-present. If, then, central government was always concerned to provide a mode of decision-making other
than through the judicial system, why did it not concede the right to
the citizen to have his criminal as well as his civil liability tested in a
form of tribunal that was not absolute? Even here, in its criminal justice
obligations, central government concedes a fair trial for crime not as an
option, but as optimal. It has long been a part of the criminal process
that in the case of hybrid offences before the magistracy, the accused is
permitted to elect to be tried in the Crown Court before a jury. While
Government has on occasions sought to abolish this route of criminality, mainly on the grounds of the saving of cost in barring access to the
jury system, the choice should exist, assuming the case-load is not too
great a burden.

There is also the questionable right of the accused in serious criminal
offences to waive trial by jury. Primarily, the concept of waiver is inap-
plicable in the case of indictable crime, although the idea of 'Bench trial'
is available in many parts of the US, and is also being adopted in those
parts of the Commonwealth that still employ the English system of jury
trial. There is nothing objectionable to the right of an offender to opt
to be tried other than by a jury. It would, of course, need to be closely
regulated by the administrators of criminal justice. Other than where
the offender opts genuinely for trial by jury, the serious offender must be
tried by a professional judge, supplemented in some instances by expert
persons.

Index